C000047623

Theatre Translation

Bloomsbury Advances In Translation Series

Series Editor:

Jeremy Munday, Centre for Translation Studies, University of Leeds, UK

Bloomsbury Advances in Translation publishes cutting-edge research in the fields of translation studies. This field has grown in importance in the modern, globalized world, with international translation between languages a daily occurrence. Research into the practices, processes and theory of translation is essential and this series aims to showcase the best in international academic and professional output.

A full list of titles in the series can be found at:
https://www.bloomsbury.com/uk/series/bloomsbury-advances-in-translation

Recent titles in the series include:

Celebrity Translation in British Theatre
Robert Stock

Extending the Scope of Corpus-Based Translation Studies
Edited by Sylviane Granger and Marie-Aude Lefer

Genetic Translation Studies
Edited by Ariadne Nunes, Joana Moura and Marta Pacheco Pinto

Institutional Translation for International Governance
Fernando Prieto Ramos

Intercultural Crisis Communication
Edited by Federico M. Federici and Christophe Declercq

Sociologies of Poetry Translation
Edited by Jacob Blakesley

Systemic Functional Linguistics and Translation Studies
Edited by Mira Kim, Jeremy Munday, Zhenhua Wang and Pin Wang

Telling the Story of Translation
Judith Woodsworth

The Pragmatic Translator
Massimiliano Morini

Translating in Town
Edited by Lieven D'hulst and Kaisa Koskinen

Theatre Translation

Theory and Practice

Massimiliano Morini

BLOOMSBURY ACADEMIC
LONDON · NEW YORK · OXFORD · NEW DELHI · SYDNEY

BLOOMSBURY ACADEMIC
Bloomsbury Publishing Plc
50 Bedford Square, London, WC1B 3DP, UK
1385 Broadway, New York, NY 10018, USA
29 Earlsfort Terrace, Dublin 2, Ireland

BLOOMSBURY, BLOOMSBURY ACADEMIC and the Diana logo
are trademarks of Bloomsbury Publishing Plc

First published in Great Britain 2022

ISBN: HB: 978-1-3501-9562-2
        ePDF: 978-1-3501-9563-9
        eBook: 978-1-3501-9564-6

Series: Bloomsbury Advances in Translation

Typeset by Integra Software Services Pvt. Ltd.

To find out more about our authors and books visit www.bloomsbury.com
and sign up for our newsletters.

Contents

List of Figures

Acknowledgements

A number of people have contributed in various ways to the making of *Theatre Translation*. Romana Zacchi has introduced me to theatre semiotics, and helped me revise Part I; she and Roberta Mullini have also filled me in on specific aspects of theatre and theatre translation history. Long before I thought of theorizing on theatre translation, Valentina Poggi set me to work on doing it. Paola Venturi has given me valuable advice on how to organize the contents, and helped with French accents. Giuseppe Ghini has discussed questions of Russian literary and theatre translation with me, normally over coffee. Raffaella Baccolini, Paolo De Lorenzi and the Centro Diego Fabbri have provided opportunities to get acquainted with mainstream drama (by asking me to give a series of talks which were moderated by Anna Luisa Santinelli). Claudio Angelini and Città di Ebla have brought contemporary experimental theatre to my hometown by means of the Ipercorpo Festival, and Claudio has put me in contact with the very kind and talented people of Agrupación Señor Serrano. Giovanni Iamartino, Massimo Sturiale, Francesca Lorandini, Pavel Drábek and Klára Škrobánková, the *Cahiers Élisabéthains*, *Theatralia* and the Modern Humanities Research Association (MHRA) have encouraged, listened to and published the results of my research on the *Pastor fido* translations. Brenda M. Hosington and Marie Alice Belle have invited me to take part in a Renaissance Society of America panel on early modern indirect translation, thus forcing me to clarify my thoughts on the matter. Jeremy Munday and Andrew Wardell have listened to my proposal with enthusiasm; Andrew, with Morwenna Scott, has guided the book to completion with patience.

Introduction: What this book is about

In Isaac Asimov's story *Nightfall* (1941), a whole world is plunged into literal and metaphorical darkness once every two thousand years. Living in a multiple-star system, the inhabitants of the planet Lagash are not used to total obscurity, and experiments have shown that people exposed to it for more than fifteen minutes can suffer very serious mental consequences. Unbeknownst to Lagash's scientific community, however, a complex solar conjunction produces a total eclipse once every two millennia. As vaguely figured in a number of quasi-religious myths, everybody goes mad while this eclipse lasts: people light fires everywhere and end up destroying most of their own civilization. After the eclipse, the cycle begins afresh, and there is a strong chance that everybody will have forgotten by the time the next disaster strikes.

Barring the destructive consequences, chronicling the history of theatrical translation theory can sometimes remind one of Asimov's story: for more than two millennia, theatrical professionals have been exchanging plots, characters and lines of dialogue across languages and cultures, but they have done so with little or no interest for theory. Whenever they have tried to conceptualize what they were doing, they have done so in apparent ignorance of their predecessors – as if a complex alignment of stars had eclipsed all former efforts in the same craft. Even in the second half of the twentieth century, when theoreticians did begin to discuss theatre translation more frequently, they tended to reiterate their conviction that they were (among) the first to do so, and that this made their positions particularly difficult. From the 1980s onwards, at a time when general Translation Studies was burgeoning, those who busied themselves with theatrical matters still had the feeling that their particular field was a barren one, and that this barrenness was connected to the difficult task of the theatre translator. As Susan Bassnett put it as late as 1998:

In terms of Translation Studies, theatre translation has always been the poor
relation, and I have tried to suggest that part of the explanation of this lies in
the impossible task that has been set for the theatre translator to accomplish.
But it is also the case that we know woefully little about the genealogy
of theatre translation in comparison with the history of other types of
translation, and this needs to be rectified. Translation specialists need to
work more closely with theatre historians, and there is a great potential for
further research in this neglected area.

(Bassnett 1998: 107)

The moment in which these sentences were written makes their tone –
despairing yet hopeful, disgruntled yet proactive – particularly appropriate. At
the turn of the millennium, Theatrical Translation Studies had known at least
two decades of intensive pioneering work, much of it influenced by theatre
semiotics and more than a little done by Bassnett herself. On the other hand,
many of the works on its performative aspects had still to be written, and
would only see the light from the year 2000 onwards. By 1998, a lot of studies
had been published on the unique position of the theatre translator, who
has to work on a text while simultaneously keeping track of its effectiveness
on stage. After 1998, and particularly in the 2010s, a lot of important work
would be done on how bringing translations on stage can be seen as a complex
collaborative effort, one in which a whole theatrical team – rather than a
unique creative individual – has a hand. More generally, if there may have
been a touch of excessive pessimism in Bassnett's assertion that theatrical
translation theory in 1998 was the 'poor relation' of (capitalized) Translation
Studies, it is certainly true that the last two decades have seen a flowering of
historical monographs, theoretical articles and collections of essays on the
subject. While there is surely a lot of 'further research' to be done, the area can
no longer be characterized as 'neglected' (see, for instance, Marinetti 2013a:
307–9). In fact, it could be argued that after so much work in so many different
directions, it is now time for a summary (see Schultze 1987; Serón-Ordóñez
2013, 2014) and a systematization.

The present monograph has been written with that aim in mind. In order
to dispel the sense of post-eclipse novelty experienced by many researchers
in the field, it seemed necessary to fix in a single volume the state of the
art at this moment in time, and to demonstrate that this state is the neat

result of concomitant (if not always concerted) efforts. Part I is dedicated to showing how theatrical translation theory has evolved from the last quarter of the twentieth century to the opening decades of the twenty-first, with an introductory chapter which summarizes two millennia of very sketchy and non-systematic thinking. Part II takes stock of current views within Theatrical Translation Studies to propose a working definition of theatre translation. Part III applies the terminology and methodology proposed in Part II to the analysis of various theatre translations, ranging from dramatic to stage-oriented versions, from Renaissance plays to contemporary experimental performances.

Even though the central part is dedicated to proposing a methodology, one preliminary terminological clarification is necessary. Attentive readers may have noticed that in the above paragraph, the labels 'theatrical translation theory', 'Theatrical Translation Studies' and 'theatre translation' are used with seeming indifference to their different shades of meaning. The indifference, however, is but a semblance, and all three terms are necessary. 'Theatrical translation theory' designates all historical views on translation, and particularly those developed by thinkers and scholars operating before the birth, or outside the borders, of Translation Studies as an academic discipline. Theatrical Translation Studies is the sub-branch of that discipline that busies itself with theatrical matters. 'Theatre translation' is the name employed by a number of scholars, and in the present monograph, to refer to the complex set of operations required to carry a theatrical spectacle across from one place and one culture to another. The process is defined with more precision in what follows; for the time being, suffice to say that it is generally semiotic rather than merely linguistic in nature, and that it involves textual translators, producers, actors and other agents of theatrical transmission.

Though *Theatre Translation* does not pretend to report on theatre translation or theatrical translation theories everywhere and at all times, it does have a chronological pattern: from this point of view, each theoretical chapter can be paired with a corresponding practical chapter (see Figure 1). Chapter 1 tells the story of how theatre translation, a performance-centric activity in Roman times, came to be regarded as a text-centric activity after humanism and continued to be studied merely as dramatic translation at least until the 1970s; it finds its practical mirror-image in Chapter 6, which details the

European diffusion of Guarini's *Pastor fido* as a poetic rather than a theatrical masterpiece. Chapter 2 expounds the 'problematic' views of such theorists as Susan Bassnett and Ortrun Zuber, caught between the gravitational pull of the dramatic text and the realization that theatre translation does not happen on the page alone; it finds its practical parallel in Chapter 7, in which a couple of contemporary Italian productions are seen to display an interesting mixture of performance-focused solutions and text-centric justifications. Chapter 3 is dedicated to recent performance-centric views of theatre translations, and Chapter 8 describes a few contemporary productions in which linguistic translation is only a part (often quite a minor one) of the sum of transformations happening on stage. The only section of the book which does not precisely fit into this pattern is Chapter 4, which provides a brief but necessary overview of Theatre Studies, insofar as that discipline has influenced Theatrical Translation Studies. The other outlier, in structural terms, is of course Part II/Chapter 5 – but that section is to be considered as an epistemological bridge. On the one hand, it provides a unifying methodology that can be seen as the net result of the theoretical progress recounted in Part I; on the other, it proposes to adopt that methodology, and its attendant terminology, for the analyses of Part III.

If the drawback of a lot of research on theatre translation is that it poses as problematic, tentative or non-systematic, the opposite defect of *Theatre Translation* may be that it has pretensions to a definitiveness of approach. In that respect, this book is destined to fail: every single scholarly effort is just a step towards further, more complete efforts which are themselves destined to be superseded; and any authors presenting their work as definitive, or even as new, must be conscious of the ironies they are visiting upon themselves. However, as a partial defence from those inevitable ironies, I will state again that this monograph is only definitive with regard to the present state of the art in the field of Theatrical Translation Studies. Its aim is to provide a map and a condensed history of what is already there, for any researcher who might wish to reconnoitre the ground after the next multisolar eclipse.

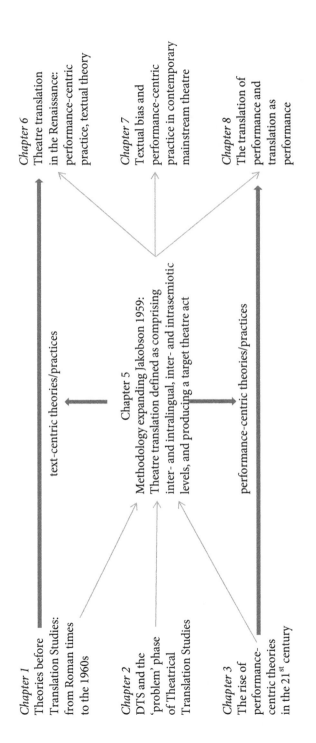

Figure 1 Theoretical framework of the book.

Part I

Theory

1

The translation of theatre before Translation Studies

Up to the late twentieth and early twenty-first centuries, there is very little in translation theory that is directly related to dramatic writing and theatrical activity. It is sufficient to scroll through any historical anthology (such as Robinson 1997) to discover that the bulk of theory is developed by thinkers and practitioners whose chosen fields were oratory (Cicero), poetry (Horace, John Dryden, the German romantics), philosophy (Leonardo Bruni) or religion (Jerome, William Tyndale, Martin Luther). When dramatic writing gets mentioned by some of these theorists, it is usually as a literary category rather than as the starting point for performance.

In this apparently barren panorama, however, it must be noted that theatre translation is a very ancient activity, and that in the Roman world there are testimonies of some kind of reflection on its processes and results which pre-date Cicero's famous pronouncements in *De optimo genere oratorum* (*c.* 46 BC) by more than a century. If this reflection (§1.1) cannot be said to amount to a full-fledged theory of translation, it is worth remembering that Cicero's own translational thinking was episodic and tangential, and that no actual theory of translation was formulated in the West until Leonardo Bruni and the early fifteenth century.

It was at that time, and during the Renaissance, that a heavily text-centric (and quite often source-oriented) view of translation was developed by humanist thinkers and rapidly accepted throughout Europe (§1.2). The central tenet of this theory is that when converting a text from one language to another, the translator has to recreate the elocution but leave the invention and disposition of the source intact. In the field of theatre translation, this meant that while many playwrights continued to freely appropriate their sources, these appropriations could not be considered as proper translations – and therefore, whenever a theatre translation got published, the emphasis was on its relationship with – and dependence on – its textual source (§1.2, 1.3). This state of affairs remained virtually unchanged until the 1950s and 1960s, when translation theory began to metamorphose into an academic discipline. At this time, while linguists and computer scientists were attempting to do away with human translators, the theorists of literary translation were only tangentially interested in theatre translation – and even then, mostly in its textual manifestations (§ 1.4).

1.1 Performance-centric beginnings: Roman practices and theories

It is quite probable that the earliest recorded instances of theatrical production in Rome were translations from the Greek (Albini and Petrone 1992: 433; Brown 1995: 49–50). Whether or not that is the case, it is certain that from the late third century to the first half of the second century BC, a great number of Greek texts were translated and brought to the Latin stage, many of these belonging to New Attic Comedy – a relatively recent genre (*c*. 320–260 BC) which focused on private rather than public life, and whose best-known authors were Menander, Philemon and Diphilus. In Rome, Plautus (*c*. 254–184 BC) and Terence (195/185–*c*. 159? BC) borrowed themes, plots, characters and often lines from these Greek works, thus producing *fabulae palliatae*, i.e. Roman plays set in Greece.

Plautus and Terence were different playwrights working at different times – the former being more inclined to farce and more linguistically and metrically inventive, the latter a more cultured and less explosive kind of writer. Given this distance and these differences, it is all the more significant that they both treated their Greek sources in much the same manner, at least if contemporary sources – and the playwrights themselves – are to be believed. Though very little is left of the Greek plays that Plautus used as starting points for his own, he 'is credited at least with formal changes, structural modifications, the elaboration of stock characters, the addition of metatheatrical elements and the insertion of Roman touches' (Manuwald 2011: 229); and the one Greek fragment that can actually be compared to a passage from Plautus' *Bacchides* shows that even when he retained the general sense, the Roman playwright brought modifications which were relevant both on the micro-linguistic and macro-theatrical levels of performance (Manuwald 2011: 229–30). Analogously, and with stronger textual evidence, it can be said that Terence used his sources rather freely in order to create new plays that would be effective on the Roman stage (Terentius 1989: 10): on occasion, for instance, he condensed two of Menander's comedies into one of his own; or, even more spuriously, he used a Greek source but also took his bearings from preceding Latin treatments by Plautus and Gnaeus Naevius (Terentius 1989: 264). In short, both playwrights can be said to be theatre translators in a performance-centric sense: they used all materials at their disposal in order to create a spectacle that would gain them popular success (Plautus) and/or erudite praise (Terence).[1]

That these two playwrights considered themselves translators is evident from what they wrote about their art. Plautus usually concluded his prologues by declaring that the play was dependent on a certain Greek source: in his *Trinummus*, for instance, he had the actor speaking the lines say that 'this was written by Philemon and translated by Plautus into Barbarian' ('Philemo scripsit, Plautus vortit barbare'; Plautus 1784: 6).[2] As for Terence, what we know about the mixing and matching techniques outlined above also depends on our knowledge of his prologues, where he felt he had to defend himself against those who accused him of contaminating too much ('isti […] disputant / contaminari non decere fabulas'; 'they say that contaminating is not decorous in plays'; Terentius 1989: 10; McElduff 2013: 87–9), as well as those who had noted his borrowings from former Latin authors ('magistratus […] exclamat furem, non poetam fabulam / dedisse'; 'the appointed magistrate exclaims that it was a thief, not a poet, that presented the play'; Terentius 1989: 264). However, while he was defensive about his use of sources, Terence was, like Plautus, completely open about the fact that his plays were translations of Greek originals ('Graeca est – Menandru'; 'this play is Greek and belongs to Menander'; Terentius 1989: 135).

It is also important to note, however, that Plautus and Terence were both considered playwrights in their own right, as well as translators – and Terence certainly presented himself as an author in his prologues, where he often complained about accusations of plagiarism or wrongly assumed authorship (Terentius 1989: 138).[3] In Rome, the *translatio* of Greek culture and literature was so wholesale and central to the canon that it could be seen to amount to original writing (Lockwood 1918: 1–3; Even-Zohar 2000: 193; McElduff 2013) – and with such performance-driven translations of Greek plays mixing and matching scenes from different sources, implanting Roman situations and characters into Attic settings, the conflation of the roles must have been even easier. In point of fact, there is plenty of evidence that even in the following centuries, Roman culture continued to see these writers as serving both a foreign master and themselves. Between the first and second centuries AD, for instance, Suetonius characterized Terence as the author of six comedies ('scripsit comoedias sex'; Suetonius 1914: 454), the beginning of whose *Adelphoe* was rated by Varro above that of Menander's comedy of the same title ('nam "Adelphorum" principium Varro etiam praefert principio Menandri'; Suetonius 1914: 456). On the other hand, Suetonius goes on to report that Cicero had a high opinion of the playwright as the translator who alone had been able to give Menander a Latin voice:

> Tu quoque, qui solus lecto sermone, Terenti,
> Conversum expressumque Latina voce Menandrum
> In medium nobis sedatis vocibus effers,
> Quiddam come loquens atque omnia dulcia dicens. (Suetonius 1914: 463)

> Only you, Terence, with your high style
> Convert and express Menander in a Latin voice
> In our midst, with your quiet utterance,
> With a certain grace and a sweetness in every word.[4]

What is particularly interesting here is the insistence on 'voice' ('Latina voce'; 'sedatis vocibus'), which prefigures the interest in the quality of 'speakability' displayed by a lot of twentieth-century theory (see, for instance, Snell-Hornby 1984; Mateo 1994). It must not be forgotten that this is the same Cicero who proclaimed that he would, in his versions of Greek public speeches, attempt to preserve the rhetorical force (*vim*) of the source words rather than the words themselves, and that he would not count the source words in his readers' hands like coins, but pay them their weight in gold (*verba appendere*, rather than *enumerare*; Cicero 1973: 41). In the Roman world,[5] translating was posited at the interface between creativity and imitation, and was always seen in performative terms – whether the arena in which the translators had to prove their mettle was a podium, a marketplace or the public theatre. It is, therefore, not surprising that such translating techniques as those of Plautus and Terence were allowed, and that these writers were considered to be both original playwrights and translators.[6]

1.2 A text-centric theory of translation: Humanism and the Renaissance

Though its textual traces are relatively rare, it seems safe to affirm that the stage- and audience-centric approach observed in Plautus and Terence continued until the end of the ancient Graeco-Roman world: a Byzantine tragedy called *Christos Paschon*, for instance, variously dated from the fourth to the eleventh century, derives the greater part of its text from seven plays by Euripides, and is actually the modern source for many Euripidean passages (Sticca 1974: 26). Just like Plautus or Terence, the author of this late classical and biblical pastiche had no hesitation in putting his ancient Greek sources to the service of his own vision, and would probably have had no great interest in discriminating between passages of translated and original writing.

After the collapse of the Roman Empire in the West, however, theatrical activity became submerged – and while there is evidence for the existence of travelling groups of players in the early Middle Ages (mainly from Christian authorities that were radically opposed to their activity; Brockett and Hildy 2003: 75; Mullini and Zacchi 2003: 16), very little is known about their repertoire. It is, therefore, impossible to trace the history of theatre translation theory between Roman times and the early Renaissance: even in the late Middle Ages, when liturgical and mystery plays began to be produced, the only reason why these could be called translations was a general reliance on biblical sources (Molinari 1983: 67–85; Mullini and Zacchi 2003: 16–21; Happé and Hüsken 2016).[7]

Between the fourth and the fifteenth centuries, as a matter of fact, very little translation theory was produced in the West in any field. The few practitioners who commented on their own or others' activity were either religious translators or, when humanism set in, translators of serious philosophical works and respected epic literature. This meant that translation theory, which had arguably been performance-centric and target-oriented in the Roman world, became heavily text-centric and source-oriented in Christian Europe. Towards the end of the fourth century, Jerome interpreted Cicero's comments on his own versions from the Greek as a defence of 'sensum [...] de sensu' translation, and praised Terence and Plautus for their free versions of Greek theatre – but then added that in rendering Scripture, even word order is a mystery ('et verborum ordo mysterium est'; Migne 1859: Hieronymus LVII, v). Ten centuries later, the Italian humanist Leonardo Bruni produced a treatise called 'On the Correct Way to Translate' (*De interpretatione recta*; c. 1426) that castigated earlier translators of Aristotle for their omissions and imprecisions, and propounded his own more painstaking philological methods (Bruni 1996: 152, 160, 162; Morini 2006: 9–10). Between the fifteenth and sixteenth centuries, Europeans began translating Virgil in their several vernaculars – mostly with a degree of attention to detail which was unprecedented for secular literature (Morini 2013a). In all these cases, the translators showed (and often declared) an awed respect for their source texts which was a very far cry from the liberties taken by Cicero with his Greek orators – not to mention the cutting-and-pasting techniques displayed by the Roman playwrights.

In this context, it comes as no surprise to learn that when people start translating theatre again, and comment on their own efforts, the emphasis is textual rather than performative. Many of the theatre translations that went into print in the Renaissance were, after all, guided by the same impulse that drove Leonardo Bruni, who translated Greek philosophy into Latin to make ancient knowledge available for the contemporary scientific community. One of the earliest and most famous theatre translations of the period, for instance, is Erasmus' Latin edition of two tragedies by Euripides (*Hecuba* and *Iphigenia in Aulis*; completed 1502–6, published in Paris in 1507 and by Manutius in 1508). These versions would then go on to be translated in the various vernaculars and staged, either in Latin or in the modern tongues, all over Europe – but there is no trace of a performance-centric intent in the learned translator's presentation of his works. Erasmus writes that he has dabbled with Euripides in order to practise his Greek (McCallum-Barry 2004: 52), and it is arguable that he decided to produce a Latin version of the Greek playwright's work for pedagogical reasons (Wilson 1973: 87). These sentiments and intentions are echoed by Latin and vernacular theatre translators throughout

Europe: many of the Senecan 'Englishers', for instance, declare in their very
title pages that they embarked on their enterprises 'for the profit of young
schollers' (Heywood 1561; see also Braden 2010a; for similar treatments of
Seneca in the rest of Europe, see Ziosi 2007). The same fate was incurred by
Roman comedy: Maurice Kyffin, for instance, defended his choice of Terence's
Andria as translating material by praising the purity of the Latin playwright's
style, and added to his paratexts the preface 'To all young Students of the Latin
tong (for whose onely help and benefit this Comoedie is published)' (Kyffin
1588: sig. A3; see also Braden 2010b). In all of these versions there is little or no
mention of performance, or of any alterations to the text that have been made
with a view to presenting the play on stage.[8]

This general text-centric tendency is reflected in the most important
pedagogical and literary treatises of the day, all of which categorize theatrical
writing as a literary genre and generally define the playwright as a poet.[9] In
Roger Ascham's *The Scholemaster*, for instance, Plautus' and Terence's plays
are considered as appropriate learning material rather than theatrical works,
their lines to be usefully turned into English like those of any other Latin
poet (Ascham 1570: 15, 31). The same attitude is found in works on literary
language and poetics. Joachim du Bellay, in his *Défense et illustration de la
langue française*, includes theatrical writing in his section on 'which kinds of
poems the French poet must choose' ('Quelz genres de Poëmes, doite elire le
Poëte Francoys'), where choosing involves not only genre but also the models
and source texts which are appropriate for imitation, and invariably hail from
the classical world (Du Bellay 1549: 27v, 29r). In England, both Sidney, in
his impassioned *Defence of Poesie* (before 1583), and Puttenham, in his more
technical *Arte of English Poesie* (1589), treat comedies and tragedies as special
cases of poetical writing which happen to be intended for the stage.

All this does not mean, of course, that plays were only meant to be read:
on the contrary, the theatre flourished again throughout Europe during the
Renaissance, and people like Du Bellay, Sidney and Puttenham were well aware
that this particular form of 'poetry' was also spoken on stage (see, for instance,
Du Bellay 1549: 29r; Sidney 1966: 65; Puttenham 1589: 20). In Spain, Italy,
France and England in particular, theatrical activity was robust and varied,
embracing as it did the world of popular entertainment as well as the courtly
sphere, not to mention private performances in aristocratic houses (Helou

2003: 27) and the academic circles where classical works were staged in Latin and Greek (Helou 2003: 17;[10] Saudis 2015). Just as happened in other forms of fictional writing, many of the plays that were being staged were translations – with the balance between original and derivative writing decidedly tilting towards the latter in the less culturally powerful areas (Prandoni 2019). Also, 'original' playwrights like Shakespeare freely appropriated bits and pieces from innumerable texts and traditions, acting like de facto interlingual or intralingual translators. However, when actual translations got published, and when their authors decided to comment on them in writing, the emphasis was almost invariably on textual fidelity rather than performative efficacy. A good example of this is offered by the many European translations of Giovan Battista Guarini's *Pastor fido* (1590; see chapter six): even those versions which were arguably or explicitly conceived for the stage, like the 1602 Dymock edition or the Spanish version by Suárez de Figueroa (1602, 1609), make no performance-centric claims in their paratexts. Suárez de Figueroa, for instance, laments the fate of the translator who has to 'paint from the life rather than at his pleasure' ('retratar al vivo y no pintar a gusto'), though he himself claims that the tragicomedy was acted out at least once in front of a courtly audience (Suárez de Figueroa 2007: 13, 276). Thus, whether or not translators have some actual or potential performance in mind, their explicit theoretical bias is textual and source-bound.

1.3 From the Renaissance to the Romantic period: Theatre, text, canon

After the Renaissance, and with the cultural impact of humanistic notions of language, translation was identified as a form of 'contrastive rhetoric', as L. G. Kelly (1979: 223) has it. Up to the late twentieth century, the idea prevailed that translators had to leave the *inventio* and *dispositio* of the source text alone and recreate its *elocutio* as skilfully as their abilities and the qualities of the target language would allow. In theory, this meant that in a novel or an epic poem, for instance, no character could be added or left out, no section of the plot altered or displaced. Of course, the field of elocution being ample, there was still scope for creativity, so that single theorists could advocate lexical and syntactic adherence on the one hand, or 'elegant unfaithfulness', the 'recreation' of the 'spirit' of the original, on the other (see, for instance, Lawrence Venuti (1995: 48–51) on D'Ablancourt and Denham). The very terms in which the question was posed are a reminder that throughout this period the kind of translation that was at the centre of the theoretical debate was the interlingual transformation of literary texts – including dramatic works, almost invariably considered in their textual dimension.

A good example of this theoretical climate is one of the very few book-length European treatises in the field, Alexander Tytler's *Essay on the Principles of Translation* (1791). Tytler's subject is clearly literary translation, or at any rate the translation of great authors, from Cicero to Cervantes. His position is the humanistic-rhetorical one outlined above, with a fine middle line drawn between the idea of careful reproduction and skilful recreation of the source author's elocution. In his opinion, a translation 'should give a complete transcript of the ideas of the original work', with a 'style and manner of writing [...] of the same character with that of the original', and 'all the ease of original composition' (Tytler 1907: 9).

Of course, obtaining that 'ease of original composition' entails a certain degree of creative liberty – so much of it, in fact, that Lawrence Venuti has counted Tytler among the proponents of fluent, 'domesticating' translation (Venuti 1995: 68–75). However, this liberty is still not comparable with the 're-creative' freedom enjoyed by Plautus and Terence, who could cut, add and paste at will. This is neatly shown in a chapter on 'good Taste in poetical Translation', which includes 'Fragments of the Greek Dramatists by Mr. Cumberland'. Tytler's brief analysis of these passages is analogous in outlook and terminology to his preceding judgements on lyrical and epic poetry: the translator 'beautifully illustrates the moral uses of tragic drama', or gives 'a very favourable idea of the spirit of the dialogue' (Tytler 1907: 91–2). Nowhere is any thought given to the suitableness of Cumberland's blank verse for the contemporary stage: clearly, these lines are considered in terms of their appropriateness as literary translation.

Tytler's text-centric approach to dramatic verse becomes even more evident when he considers – in a passage bearing the deontic title 'The genius of the translator should be akin to that of the original author' – Voltaire's 1734 version of Hamlet's most famous soliloquy. Perhaps fired by nationalistic pride as well as source-oriented bias, Tytler's language here becomes more moralistic than elsewhere, as he indignantly asks 'who gave Mr. Voltaire a right thus to transmute the pious and superstitious Hamlet into a modern *philosophe* and *Esprit fort*', and wonders whether this should be called 'a translation from Shakespeare' at all (Tytler 1907: 210–11). The verb 'transmute' is used with a strongly negative connotation here, as is 'metamorphosed' in the following passage. Evidently, so much target-oriented change turns Voltaire's text into something 'disfigured', rather than a translation:

> Voltaire, in his essay *sur la Tragédie Angloise*, has chosen the famous soliloquy in the tragedy of Hamlet [...] as one of those striking passages which best exemplify the genius of Shakespeare, and which, in the words of the French author, *demandent grace pour toutes ses fautes*. It may therefore be presumed, that the translator in this instance endeavoured, as far as lay in his power, not only to adopt the spirit of his author, but to represent him as favourably as possible to his countrymen. Yet, how wonderfully has he metamorphosed, how miserably disfigured him! In the original, we have the perfect picture of a mind deeply agitated [...] In the translation, we have a formal and connected harangue, in which it would appear, that the author, offended with the abrupt manner of the original, and judging those irregular starts of expression to be unsuitable to that precision which is required in abstract reasoning, has corrected, as he thought, those defects of the original, and given union, strength, and precision, to this philosophical argument.
>
> (Tytler 1907: 207–8)

The prevalence of this kind of textual bias is never questioned between the Renaissance and the late twentieth century – and theatre translators often betray their uneasy awareness of this state of affairs. More or less when Tytler was writing his *Essay*, Jean-François Ducis was recreating Shakespeare for a popular French audience used to neoclassical tragedies (Heylen 1993: 26–44). Working on existing French translations, Ducis tried to make the plays as palatable as possible to his audience. In his *Macbeth*, for instance, the titular character appears to reconcile himself with God and his destiny before he dies (Ducis 1827: 205), and the banquet is not shown because gluttony was thought unsuitable for tragedy. In his 'Avertissement' to the printed version of the tragedy, Ducis declares that after his previous successes in this field, he was tempted to make the most terrifying of Shakespearean plays known to the public ('j'ai été tenté d'y faire connaître [...] la plus terrible de ses productions dramatiques'). 'As to the manner in which I have treated [...] this terrifying subject', he goes on, 'the reader will see what belongs to me, and what I owe to Shakespeare' ('Quant à la manière don't j'ai traité le fond de ce sujet vraiment terrible, le lecteur verra ce qui m'appartient, et ce que je dois à Shakespeare'); and he adds that everybody has Le Tourneur's translation in their hands, so they can form their own idea on the matter ('la traduction de M. Le Tourneur est entre les mains de tout le monde'; Ducis 1827: 121–2). Prudently, he refrains from openly stating that his version is a translation – yet he mentions the translation that it was based on, so that he can also avoid presenting this *Macbeth* as his own work.

Ducis' prudence reflects the plight of theatre translation in modern Europe: on the one hand, playwrights do create performance-driven translations which adapt their source texts to a new staging situation; on the other, they know that their translations cannot quite pass muster as proper ones on the page. In theoretical terms, theatrical versions have been subsumed under literary translation, and the textual strictures of the latter have been imposed upon the former.

Almost invariably, what makes these strictures even more binding is that whenever theatrical writing gets mentioned in the debate on translation theory, this is because the source playwright is a canonical author. Shakespeare, again, is the perfect example of this situation. On the one hand, between the eighteenth and nineteenth centuries he was performed all over Europe, quite often with remarkable disregard for the letter of his texts; the Ducis versions, for instance, were initially used as sources in most theatrical traditions (Lambert 1993; Levin 1993; Schultze 1993; and see Kofler 2013 on German 'adaptations'). On the other hand, by the time Shakespeare's plays travelled from one European country to another, both in book form and on stage, Shakespeare had already become the great northern Bard, and the object of a literary cult even outside Britain (Dobson 1992; Dávidházi 1993). Therefore, performance-driven though many actual translations were, when translation theory busied itself with Shakespeare, it always did so in text-centric as well as strongly source-oriented terms.

One of Shakespeare's most famous European translators, August Wilhelm Schlegel, exemplified this duality in a long article he published in 1796, at the beginning of his work on the Renaissance playwright. In 'Something on William Shakespeare, on the occasion of [the publication of Goethe's] Wilhelm Meister', Schlegel acknowledges the importance of his predecessor, Wieland, who first took upon himself the 'Herculean labour' ('herkulische Arbeit') of converting many of the plays into German ('verdeutschen'). Wieland's pioneering versions, flawed though they were due to the scant knowledge of English then current in Germany, were fundamental not only in literary terms but also because they contributed to creating a new theatrical taste. 'Who would then have dared to imagine', Schlegel writes, 'that such pagan, unruly, barbaric plays [...] would ever have been allowed to be shown before our eyes', and end up obscuring the star of French tragic art? ('Wer hätte's sich's damals einbilden dürfen, daß so heidnisch regellose, barbarische Stücke [...] uns jemahls würden vor die Augen gebracht werden dürfen?'; Schlegel 1796: 76; Lefevere 1977: 48–9). The ascent of Shakespeare, Schlegel adds, was much helped by Lessing, who not only praised the English playwright but wrote dramatic works – like *Emilia Galotti* – which helped increase his countrymen's receptivity to Shakespeare on stage.

If Schlegel knows very well that the main purpose of translating Shakespeare is preparing his texts for the stage, however, the praise he has for the author, and the things he has to say about the translator's task, are decidedly text-centric. This is particularly evident in the following passage, in which he explains why he is convinced that the English playwright should now be re-translated:

> Readers of Shakespeare who have passed all the tests described above [i.e., who can read him in English] would not be adverse, for the sake of change, to rest now and again on their own soil in the shadow of his works, if those works could be transplanted without too great a loss of their beautiful leafwork. Would it therefore not be a very good thing if we had a translation? 'But we have one already, and it is complete, and faithful, and good.' So it is! We had to have that much to be able to wish for more. The desire for luxury follows the satisfaction of basic needs; now the best in this field is no longer good enough for us. If Shakespeare could and should only be translated into prose, then we ought to rest content with what has been achieved so far. But he is a poet, also in the sense in which one connects this word to the use of metre. If it were possible to recreate his work faithfully and yet at the same time poetically, to follow the letter of his meaning step by step and yet to

catch part of the innumerable, indescribable marvels which lie not in the letter, but float above it like a breath of the spirit! It is worth a try.

(Schlegel 1796: 81–2; Lefevere 1977: 49–50)

According to Schlegel, it is not because the plays do not work well on stage that they should be re-translated, but because they have not been rendered in all their poetical splendour. The new versions he proposes would benefit readers, not theatregoers; and they would have to be in verse rather than prose, because Shakespeare is to be appreciated as a poet whose very syllables are important ('Allein er ist ein Dichter, auch in der Bedeutung, da man diesen Nahmen an den Gebrauch des Sylbenmaaßes knüpft').[11] The comment on the 'beautiful leafwork' of Shakespeare's writing ('schönen Blätterschmuck') is clearly a reference to elocution, i.e. the only domain of rhetoric which, according to humanists, is the province of the translator. The ultimate aim is one of faithfulness and poetical re-creation ('to recreate his work faithfully and yet at the same time poetically'; 'ihn treu und zugleich poetisch nachzubilden').

1.4 Twentieth-century theories of dramatic translation

In Germany and elsewhere, translation theory did not fundamentally change from the late eighteenth century to the first half of the twentieth. The focus of all the important contributors in this field remained firmly on translating texts. Individual or cultural preferences might be divided between target- and source-oriented translations (Schleiermacher 1816), waver between views of translation as a patriotic activity or as a form of philological criticism (Polledri 2010: 307) or go to versions capable of showing the philosophical unity of all the world's languages (Benjamin 1961: 56–69 [1923]) – but everybody tacitly agreed on the inviolability of the invention and disposition of the source text, and therefore excluded performance-driven, transformative theatre translations from their field of vision (mostly by dubbing them as adaptations). Translated playwrights, when they got mentioned by theorists at all, continued to be seen as original poets or writers rather than as people responsible for staging their works.

For a while, these attitudes remained in place when translation theory became an accepted area of academic interest after the Second World War. In the 1950s and 1960s, a lot of effort and funding was devoted to the project of producing a 'science' of translation and, if at all possible, replacing translating humans with machines – but even in this case, the focus was almost exclusively textual (Weaver 1955; Catford 1965). The same text-centric and source-bound emphasis is observable in those academics who, around the same time, write of translation as a literary and re-creative activity. The prescriptive mood of the time is neatly summarized in a short essay written in 1966 by Italian academic and translator Carlo Izzo, who invited translators to exercise 'humility' in their recreations of a quasi-sacred 'original' (Izzo 1970). When any of these scholars had something to say about theatre translation, their focus was mostly on printed plays rather than performances, and on playwrights as great authors of the European canon.

One of the most interesting figures of this period in the field of literary translation was the Czech Jiří Levý, the European peregrinations of whose works are in themselves worthy material for Translation Studies. Levý published his original *Umění Překladu* (*Art of Translation*) in 1963, arousing great interest in the community of Slavic scholars at home and abroad. A proposal for a German version followed, for which Levý produced what was essentially a new Czech book, which was sent to the translators chapter by chapter in 1967 and then published under the title *Die literarische Übersetzung: Theorie einer Kunstgattung* in 1969. By the time this edition came out, Levý was dead. When a second Czech edition was produced in 1983, therefore, it was back-translated from the 1969 German monograph – which had also spawned a Russian version in 1974 and a Serbo-Croatian one in 1982. The English edition we have today is a translation of the 1983 Czech version, itself based on the German edition which was a translation of an unpublished revision by the author (Levý 2011: xvii).

Levý is a structuralist who combines the interest in textual surfaces typical of the Prague circle with a functionalist attention to context and a penchant for close reading derived from his English studies. His analyses of translators' strategies, of the problems they are faced with, are very insightful, particularly in the domain of poetic translation. When it comes to theatre translation, Levý's standpoint is decidedly text-centric, based as it is on his purpose of creating an 'illusionist' version that poses as a new original (Levý 2011: 20). When he mentions Shakespeare, for instance, he always does so with an eye to reproducing his plays 'correctly' and castigating those who try to amend them in translation

(Levý 2011: 25, 33, 40), though on occasion he allows a certain degree of latitude when the cultural context has changed beyond recognition (Levý 2011: 44).[12] Of course, as he admits in his chapter on 'Drama Translation'/'Die Übersetzung von Theaterstücken', performance-related concepts such as speakability ('Sprechbarkeit') are fundamental in theatrical versions (Levý 1969: 141–8), and regardless of what translators do with their target texts, whole scenes or characters are often cut or altered in actual productions (Levý 1969: 158). This kind of freedom, however, seems to be the director's prerogative rather than the translator's – and even that form of re-creative liberty is allowed by Levý a little grudgingly, in light of his final comments regarding the need for the 'dramaturg' to have the source play 'to hand':

> The point is that the text is the means rather than the end (Stanislavskii said that to the actors words were not mere sounds but rather they evoked images); its individual elements contribute to the creation of scenic images to different degrees and in particular ways (it exhibits a markedly teleological hierarchy). This [*sic*] point of this remark [Sinn dieses Hinweises] is not to furnish any theoretical justification for carelessness in translation [übersetzerische Nachlässigkeit], but [sondern, im Gegenteil] to point out that it is necessary to translate, at least in some key respects, much more precisely and above all in a more carefully considered way than is usual [weit genauer und vorallem reflektierter übersetzt werden muß]. The dramaturg should in any case have the relevant original script to hand [das Original zur Hand].
>
> (Levý 2011: 166; Levý 1969: 158–9)

In this theoretical light, the performance-driven transformation of theatrical writing – including changes in terms of invention and disposition – is presented as being outside the scope of translation. It is the 'dramaturg' who can operate those alterations, while the translator 'must' exercise the utmost care and, in sharp contrast ('im Gegenteil') to what happens on stage, avoid any hint of 'carelessness'. Precision and careful consideration are of the essence: evidently, the play must not suffer any form of corruption before it gets into the slightly freer hands of the director.

A very similar position is expressed around the same time by Georges Mounin, a French linguist and semiotician who in the 1960s produced three highly valued monographs on the theory and history of translation. In *Teoria e storia della traduzione*, written in 1965 for Einaudi and published directly in Italian, Mounin dedicates a short chapter to theatre translation. Just like Levý, he acknowledges that this form of interlingual transformation happens in ways which are uniquely its own; but again, like the Czech scholar, Mounin cannot quite bring himself to call this transformative process one of translation. In his opinion, the greater alterations needed in this field are justified by the fact that plays have to be presented on stage, and the audience pronounces a 'sentence without appeal: the text either survives translation, or it does not'. However, this does entail that theatre translation can be defined in broader terms:

> This explains why theatrical translation, when it is not written for a school or scholarly edition, but for mere acting purposes ['bensì per la recitazione'], must treat the text so that it can be considered an adaptation, as well as a translation ['tanto un adattamento quanto una traduzione']. Faithfulness ['fedeltà'] to what made that play a theatrical success must be considered before faithfulness to vocabulary, grammar, syntax and even style. One must translate the theatrical value before one worries about rendering literary and poetic values, and if a conflict arises between the former and the latter, the former must take precedence.
>
> (Mounin 1965: 155)

On the face of it, this might look like a rather performance-centric view of theatre translation; but it has to be stressed that for Mounin, the process defined above is not exactly one of translation – it is a mixture of translation and adaptation. If the 'adaptive', transformative element is taken out of the combination, what remains is a rather traditional definition of translation as an elocutionary reproduction of literary and poetic values, involving 'faithfulness' to words, grammar and syntax.

2

The age of Translation Studies: Early work on theatre translation

From the late 1970s onwards, academic ideas on translation have been revolutionized by the cultural turn of Descriptive Translation Studies (§2.1). For the first time, the focus is not on the translator's task or on the translation process, but on actual translations as products of a target culture. James S. Holmes, André Lefevere, Gideon Toury and others on the 'Tel Aviv–Leuven' axis have re-shaped Translation Studies as a sociologically inclined, humanistic discipline. However, at least at the beginning, most Descriptive Translation Studies scholars concentrated their attention on texts: when theatrical writing featured in their works, it did so in the form of translated plays and their sources.

This initial textual bias makes things difficult for Susan Bassnett, the only scholar in the group whose academic interests lie firmly within the area of theatrical translation (§2.2). Herself a translator with an academic grounding in theatre semiotics, Bassnett is perfectly aware that the process cannot be reduced to its textual dimension. However, since her viewpoint is that of a single translator's (rather than the general, bird's-eye view of textual Descriptive Translation Studies), she cannot bring herself to look at theatre translations as merely facts of target cultures. With varying degrees of assurance and desperation, her studies of the 1980s and 1990s strive towards a performance-centric view but take their bearings from a text-centric position – consequently, they all tend to define the practice as problematic or labyrinthine.

Bassnett's mapping of the sub-field was very influential, and general ideas on theatre translation did not change until the beginning of the new millennium. Other studies of the 1980s and the 1990s maintain a 'problematic' outlook (§2.3) and continue to distinguish between textual translation on the one hand and performance-driven 'interpretations', 'rewritings' or 'adaptations' on the other (§2.3, 2.4), on occasion creating such hybrid terms as 'tradaptation' (§2.4). It is also important to note that the 1980s were the first decade in which it became possible to think of recording a significant number of theatrical performances (§2.3) – videotape being the earliest of a series of technological innovations which would, in time, contribute to the rise of fully performance-centric theories of theatre translation.

2.1 The name and nature of Translation Studies

Perspectives changed radically in the course of the 1970s, when a number of scholars based in Israel (Itamar Even-Zohar, Gideon Toury), Belgium (André Lefevere, Theo Hermans, José Lambert), the Netherlands (James S. Holmes) and Britain (Susan Bassnett) founded the discipline that came to be known as 'Translation Studies', or more often as 'Descriptive Translation Studies'.[1] Since most of the proponents of Descriptive Translation Studies had an academic background in comparative literature, they reinstated the translation of fictional writing at the centre of the field, thus implicitly challenging the approaches of invariance-seeking, algorithm-based linguistic research. Unlike previous literary scholars, however, the Descriptive Translation Studies group tried to avoid prescriptive pronouncements and decided to concentrate on the empirical observation of existing translations.

Nowhere is this novel approach presented with more clarity than in the founding document of the discipline, James S. Holmes' 'The Name and Nature of Translation Studies' – first presented as a conference paper in 1972, then variously revised until its posthumous publication in a 1988 collection of essays. Holmes starts out by baptizing the discipline according to its position on the map of academic research. He has no problem with the term *Übersetzungswissenschaft*, he says, because the German equivalent for science is commonly used in connection with language and literature (*Sprachwissenschaft, Literaturwissenschaft*). However, the English word 'science' is not really employed in the same combinations and risks creating a false analogy with 'harder' sciences like mathematics, physics or chemistry. Therefore, he proposes to use the English term 'Translation Studies', by analogy with other humanistic fields such as 'Russian studies, American studies, Commonwealth studies, population studies, communication studies' (Holmes 1988: 69–70). Following on from a definition given by Werner Koller, Holmes characterizes Translation Studies as an empirical discipline, and goes on to identify two main objectives and the branches that should busy themselves with their realization:

> (1) to describe the phenomena of translating and translation(s) as they manifest themselves in the world of our experience, and (2) to establish general principles by means of which these phenomena can be explained and predicted. The two branches of pure translation studies concerning themselves with these objectives can be designated *descriptive translation studies* (DTS) or *translation description* (TD) and *theoretical translation studies* (ThTS) or *translation theory* (TTh).
>
> (Holmes 1988: 71)

Holmes envisages a strict correlation between the two branches of the discipline. In the decades that followed this seminal essay, however, it was above all the descriptive branch of Translation Studies that flourished – so much so, in fact, that the whole discipline came to be known as Descriptive Translation Studies. Most of the work done in this descriptive vein had literary translation at its centre, and for the first time in history, deontic terms disappeared almost completely, leaving room for an empirical, ethically neutral discussion of translations as 'facts of target cultures' (Toury 1995: 23).

On the face of it, this climate should have been ideal for a debate on theatre translation in performance-centric terms: if translations are to be observed for what they are (as opposed to what they should be), and if it is the position they occupy in the target culture that counts, then it should be possible to discuss works such as Plautus' and Terence's, as well as Schlegel's versions of Shakespeare, in the same vein. However, it is to be noted that Descriptive Translation Studies, at least initially, was very text-oriented in outlook: its proponents busied themselves only rarely with theatre translation, and even when they did, they tended to do so in markedly – though not exclusively – text-centric terms. In 'The Name and Nature of Translation Studies', for instance, there are various mentions of literature and literary translation in general, but none of theatre translation: Holmes was a poetry expert, and many of the essays collected in *Translated!* (1988) focus on that genre. In one of the most celebrated books produced by the group, *The Manipulation of Literature* (Hermans 1985), only Susan Bassnett's essay was dedicated to 'Translating Theatre *Texts*' (italics mine). The most important books in the field produced in the 1990s, Toury's *Descriptive Translation Studies – and beyond* and Lawrence Venuti's *The Translator's Invisibility* (both published in 1995), also focused overwhelmingly on literature as something that is printed and read, rather than presented on stage.[2] Thus, if the prescriptive outlook of linguistic 'science' and earlier literary scholars was abandoned, the textual bias still applied.

A good illustration of this apparent paradox can be found in the work of one of the most brilliant scholars in the group, André Lefevere. In an article published in 1982 and mainly focusing on how the Brechtian canon has fared in the English-speaking world, Lefevere borrows the term 'refraction' from optics to cover all the ways in which an author gets assimilated into a foreign culture and language. Once again, this would appear to be a perfect theoretical framework in which to consider both textual and stage-driven translations on an equal footing – and in addition, here and elsewhere (see, for instance, Lefevere 1992: 41–58), this looser framework gives Lefevere the opportunity to make sense of theatrical versions. However, although he deliberately avoids distinguishing between 'translation' and 'adaptation' (Lefevere 1992: 47), Lefevere normally focuses his analyses on 'plays' and on what the 'reader' finds in printed translations. Here, for instance, is a list of possible refractions of a literary work:

> First of all, let us accept that refractions – the adaptation of a work of literature to a different audience, with the intention of influencing the way in which that audience reads the work – have always been with us in literature. Refractions are to be found in the obvious form of translation, or in the less obvious forms of criticism [...] commentary, historiography [...] teaching, the collection of works in anthologies, the production of plays. These refractions have been extremely influential in establishing the reputation of a writer and his or her work.
>
> (Lefevere 2000: 235)

If the logic of this passage is followed, it would appear that 'the production of plays' is to be considered not as a form of translation, but as yet another possibility in the larger category of 'refraction'. Admittedly, since Lefevere is once again concerned with the literary works that an audience 'reads', the plays he has in mind here might be those that are adapted from a novel or an epic poem, rather than from a foreign play. However, in the paragraph after this one he ascribes to the field of refraction the translations created by the drama critic Eric Bentley, who passed on Brechtian theatre to American audiences 'with all the misunderstandings and misconceptions this implies'. In the end, although Lefevere is one of the most acute observers of cultural transmission of the late twentieth century, he does not seem prepared to grant (or interested in granting) the status of translation to performance-driven theatrical rewriting.

2.2 Susan Bassnett and the 'problem' phase of theatrical translation theory

Within the Descriptive Translation Studies group, the scholar who most consistently busied herself with theatre translation was Susan Bassnett. As seen above, she was the only one who focused on theatre in the 1985 collection, *The Manipulation of Literature*. She wrote several articles on the subject in the course of the 1980s and 1990s, and dedicated a separate chapter of her 1980 monograph on *Translation Studies* to it. A mere roll-call of titles leads to a definition of her work as explorative and tentative – and, by extension, of the whole period as the 'problem' phase of theatrical translation theory. She discusses 'The Problems of Translating Theatre Texts' (Bassnett 1981, 1983) and defines the 'Strategies and Methods for Translating Theatre Texts' as 'Ways through the Labyrinth' (Bassnett 1985). She describes the problems created by theatre translation as 'Textual Complexities' (Bassnett 1990), and up until the late 1990s, she claims to be 'Still Trapped in the Labyrinth' when embarking on 'Further Reflections on Translation and Theatre' (Bassnett 1998).

Apart from 'problems' and other 'problematic' words such as 'labyrinth', the most recurrent set of terms here has to do with 'text' – which might prompt one to conclude that Bassnett's perspective is once again restricted to translated plays, rather than theatre. When one reads her articles, chapters and monograph, actually, this turns out not to be the case: Bassnett has the performative side of theatre translation constantly in mind – and it is precisely this performative side which turns out to be problematic for the translator. However, as will be seen below, the presence of the 'textual' set of keywords in her titles is not without significance, as it accurately reflects Bassnett's analytical angle: invariably, even when she is looking at the performance of translated plays, she is doing so from the viewpoint of a translator who is faced with a foreign author's words, rather than with their theatrical realization.

The performance-centric aspects of Bassnett's perspective are fundamentally derived from the semiotic theories of theatre that became fashionable in the late 1970s. In this period, French theorists like Anne Ubersfeld and Patrice Pavis started to reverse the traditional 'logocentric' vision of dramatic production (Pavis 2000: 11), which sees all performances as more or less imperfect realizations of an original playtext. According to semiotic theory, the play can no longer be simplistically 'translated' into a performance, because many things that happen in performance are neither inscribed in nor presupposed by the text. Taking their cue from theatrical practitioner-theoreticians such as Antonin Artaud and Bertolt Brecht, Pavis, Ubersfeld and others set out to explore the 'gestural' and material aspects of staged theatre (Pavis 2000: 67–76). Other semioticians and linguists, in Britain and elsewhere, defined the relationship between 'dramatic' and 'performance text' as a problematic intertextual nexus (Elam 1980: 208–9), investigated the impact of unscripted audience participation (De Marinis 1978, 1979; Elam 1980: 87–92) and analysed the pragmatic potential of theatrical writing (Serpieri 1978; Aston 1983). While different in outlook and methodology, all these works were united by a common recognition that plays could no longer be analysed in isolation from their mises-en-scène.

This performance-centric revolution could not but have consequences on the domain of theatrical translation theory. If a performance could no longer be seen as a reflection of a play, it followed that a text-centric view of theatre translation was no longer tenable. Susan Bassnett was perfectly aware of these developments (see Bassnett 1980), just as she was aware that recent functionalist theories of translation had put the emphasis on the *skopos* of the target rather than of the source text (Reiss and Vermeer 1984; Bassnett 2002: 131). What remained to be done was to find a definition for the theatre translator's plight according to the function of his/her work and this stage-oriented view of dramatic writing.

In her 1980s and 1990s contributions, Bassnett (1983: 49; 1998: 90; 2002: 119) often opens her discussions of the topic by complaining that very little has been written about it. This is generally true, as seen in the preceding chapters, but also specifically true in the burgeoning context of Descriptive Translation Studies, whose exponents, particularly in the early phases, concentrate primarily on poetry (Bassnett 1983: 49; 2002: 119). Bassnett motivates this relative neglect by mentioning the difficulties incurred by practitioner and theoretician alike in what she calls this 'most problematic [...] area of translation studies research' (Bassnett 1998: 90). She then usually proceeds to illustrate some of those difficulties, and the solutions she herself has come up with on various occasions.

The main problem for the theatre translator is that she is not working on a text that is complete in and of itself, but on something that can only realize its full potential in performance. As Anne Ubersfeld has pointed out, the playtext is *troué* – i.e. riddled with gaps which can only be filled up in performance (Bassnett 1998: 91). In 'Still Trapped in the Labyrinth', Bassnett briefly toyed with the idea of a sub-text to be deduced by performers and translators, but immediately discarded it – even if such a thing existed at all, it would end up being realized differently by each interpreter (see also Bassnett 1983: 53). Whenever a play is brought to the stage, it is transformed into a new cultural object – and the same goes for its interlingual translations: 'acculturation' is inevitable, and any statements to the contrary serve purposes of intellectual imperialism (hence the scorn Bassnett pours on Michael Frayn's suggestion that Chekhov is 'universal'; Bassnett 1998: 93–4).[3] Translators work with their own linguistic and cultural instruments, which they inevitably bring to bear on the source play – though they can still decide whether they want to produce something that sounds exotic or thoroughly domesticated (Bassnett 1998: 93).

Bassnett's awareness that every translation is a cultural transposition – and that it has a role to play in the target culture – is in evidence when she describes the work she and David Hirst did on an English version of Pirandello's stage play *Trovarsi* for BBC Radio (Bassnett 1998: 96–8). On this occasion, there were two different orders of problems that she and her co-translator had to solve: on the linguistic plane, the question was how to render the style of Italian lesser nobility without employing 'parodic language of the P. G. Wodehouse variety' (Bassnett 1998: 96); in functionalist terms, the transformation of a stage play into radio drama entailed heavy losses partly remedied by 'transposing visual effects into verbal' (Bassnett 1998: 97). This led to an English version that bore an obvious resemblance to the Italian source, but with a number of additions and alterations (including in the *dispositio* of single scenes or speeches). Unlike Levý or Mounin, however, Bassnett 'would strenuously resist the application of any term such as "adaptation" or "version" to our translation'. She insists that theatre translation has to work in this way, taking into consideration the changes in destination and culture that influence the practitioner's choices.

This is a performance-centric view of theatre translation, in that the conditions in which the target play has to be presented can lead the translator to modify the source in ways that go beyond the mere (re-)creation of elocution. Certain aspects of Bassnett's theory, however, are still decidedly text-centric, because in all her works on the subject, she applies herself to the close reading of theatrical passages and wonders how best to reproduce their effects in translation (even the Pirandello passage discussed above is a case in point; or see her discussion of *La cantatrice chauve* in Bassnett 1983: 58–9). While the target stage has its own gravitational pull, Bassnett never stops considering the source text as another, equally important, centre of gravity – particularly when the texts she considers belong to canonical or near-canonical authors (Bassnett 1983: 57; Bassnett 1998: 102–6). This is why words such as 'problem' or 'labyrinth' occur so often in her titles and her works; and this is probably why the task of the translator is described as a struggle rather than a pleasure:

> What is left for the translator to do is to engage specifically with the signs of the text: to wrestle with the deictic units, the speech rhythms, the pauses and silences, the shifts of tone or of register, the problems of intonation patterns: in short, the linguistic and paralinguistic aspects of the written text that are decodable and reencodable.
>
> (Bassnett 1998: 107)

This very interesting passage illustrates the bind in which Bassnett finds herself. As a theatre translator, she knows perfectly well that the performative nature of her profession requires a higher degree of liberty from the shackles which have been imposed on secular translators since humanism. On the other hand, as an observer of her own work and someone who is certainly in love with the source texts she is working on, she cannot really bring herself to allow that liberty to be anything but very limited. The translator must (the deontic is not expressed, but it is still implicit in 'what is left for the translator to do') analyse all the aspects of the source that can be decoded and re-encoded – not only what is actually there but also what is there potentially: the 'paralinguistic aspects of the written text'. It is not by chance that the adjective 'written' appears at this decisive moment, towards the end of the chapter: one is reminded of Levý recommending that the dramaturg work with the source script close at hand.

Ultimately, the reason for Bassnett's theoretical position remaining halfway between text- and performance-centric is her analytical angle. While from the early 1980s onwards Lefevere, Toury and others were looking at existing translations and judging them not for what they should have been but for what they actually were, Bassnett is still discussing processes rather than products. By choosing her own work as a focus, she is effectively limiting the scope of her research to the situations in which someone like her, with her own professional 'habitus' (Simeoni 1998), is translating for the theatre. Since she works primarily on texts rather than on theatrical production (with such exceptions as the BBC-produced Pirandello), her considerations cannot but be, at least partially, text-centric. In this sense, her sensation of being trapped inside the labyrinth is perfectly justified: in fact, Bassnett has chosen that position for herself, implicitly declining the opportunity to look at the labyrinth from above.

Given that theatre translation had always been, and still was, the 'poor relation' of other genres, this is not in itself surprising: the limitations and compromises in Bassnett's views are not exclusively her own, but belong to a transitional phase in the development of theatrical translation theory. During the same period, other scholars in the field were facing the same contradictions and coming up with different but equally problematic solutions.

2.3 Further problems, future solutions: Ortrun Zuber and the rise of technology

At the beginning of the 1980s, independently of Bassnett's work and most developments in Descriptive Translation Studies, another group of scholars, translation practitioners and theatre professionals attempted to investigate theatre translation in a fairly systematic way. This group gathered around Australian academic Ortrun Zuber (later Zuber-Skerritt), who between 1980 and 1984 edited two collections of essays entitled *The Languages of Theatre: Problems in the Translation and Transposition of Drama* (1980) and *Page to Stage: Theatre as Translation* (1984). As shown by the subtitle of the first book, these works belong to the 'problem' phase of theatrical translation theory: in the introduction to that collection, 'problems' is used in the very first clause and then repeated six more times in a mere forty-four lines of text. The title of the 1984 book, on the other hand, expresses some awareness of the new semiotic views on theatre: if a theatrical event is itself a 'translation' (*Page to Stage*), it follows that its translation into another language cannot be looked upon as a merely linguistic process.

Though it makes the title in 1984, this awareness is already there as an inspiration in 1980 (Gostand 1980; Zuber 1980b). In her presentation of the first collection, Zuber associates the 'problems' involved in the 'verbal and non-verbal transposition of drama from one language and cultural background to another' with those of its passage 'from the text on to the stage'. The use of the word 'transposition', as well as the specification that it can involve a change of 'cultural background', is significant: the idea, confirmed by even a quick reading of most chapters, is that this book will not be limited in scope to those cases of translation which only involve a textual recreation of the source. The inclusion of the word 'drama', however, reflects the typical bind of the 'problem phase': though the collection proposes to confront 'stage' issues, its initial focus is still on the 'page'. Zuber's list of the people who might want to read *The Languages of Theatre* is an indication of her willingness to extend the question beyond the domains of literature and translation – but also of the fact that, just like Susan Bassnett, she is still very much concentrating on processes rather than products. She hopes:

- that *those interested in drama/theatre* would wish to read some, if not all contributions,
- that *theatre groups* and translators of plays might benefit from reading about some authors' experiences in overcoming certain problems,
- that senior secondary and tertiary *students* might study the book in certain courses (e.g. English, Drama, Translation, Theatre Studies, Communication etc.) and

– that *scholars* might be stimulated to investigate similar problems in their own fields, applying the same or different methods of research. (Zuber 1980b: xiii)

Like Bassnett, Zuber points to a dearth of studies in the field ('[t]his is the first book focusing on translation problems unique to drama'), as well as to the preference of translation scholars for other forms of imaginative writing, particularly poetry. As stated in her introduction, the essays in her collection will analyse translation textually, but with an emphasis on 'non-verbal' as well as verbal aspects, and an awareness that 'a play is written for a performance and must be actable and speakable' (Zuber 1980b: xiii). Again, like Bassnett, Zuber is addressing the whole question from the standpoint of someone who is translating a play with an eye to stage production.

In the book, which is mostly academic but hosts two contributions by playwrights, the most consistent attempt at formulating a theory from this standpoint is provided not by Zuber herself but by Franz H. Link. His article on 'Translation, Adaptation and Interpretation of Dramatic Texts' is an exploration of the various forms of interventionism that come into play in theatre translation. In the opening sections, Link discusses translation in exclusively verbal terms, starting from non-dramatic fiction and considering the changes that may become necessary – intra- and interlingually – when an old-fashioned version of the language is used, when the source is written in a dialect that the target audience would be unable to understand or when cultural allusions become unidentifiable. In the case of theatre, of course, the need for other kinds of modifications may be felt, because stage conventions are historically determined and a contemporary audience may not be able to understand the material workings of Greek or Elizabethan drama.

In this article, the scene seems set for a fully performance-centric description of theatre translation. The fact that Link chooses not to consider stage directions as 'part of the dramatic text' (Link 1980: 34), for instance, is particularly interesting: directions are the author's attempt at controlling what stage managers and actors do, a textual invasion of performative space. By excluding them from view, Link is insisting on the independence of the people who create the theatrical experience in real time – but, on the other hand, he is also limiting the scope of theatre translation, as evidenced by the multiple terms he uses in his title. Link goes as far as to employ the term 'literal' for the kinds of 'drama translation' in which no great modification is needed (Link 1980: 31), and prefers the terms 'rewriting', 'adaptation' and 'interpretation' for all the interventions that take place between text and stage. Once again, the textual and performative planes are perhaps given equal dignity, but they are kept in rather strict segregation.

The same admixture, with the same sense of unresolved uneasiness, pervades the second collection edited by Zuber-Skerritt in 1984, as well as her personal contributions to that book. That performance-centric concepts of theatre translation are still in their infancy is shown by contributions written by stage professionals and translators who tend to distinguish, like Link in 1980, between literal and free translations, adaptations and versions (e.g. Nowra 1984). The editor's article on 'Translation Science and Drama Translation' betrays an understanding of translation theory that is effectively pre-Descriptive Translation Studies, notwithstanding Lefevere's contributions to this and the preceding volume. Zuber-Skerritt's theoretical notions belong to the 1960s and early 1970s (see also Zuber-Skerritt 1988): she conceives of 'Translation Science' (with capital initials) as being 'housed in pure linguistics, and based on theory' – in other words, as a discipline that can be reduced to mathematical speculation. Her problem with this concept is that she has to work on theatre translation – i.e. on something that defies any attempt at mathematical and purely linguistic definition. She adds, therefore, that just as Chomsky distinguishes between 'competence' and 'performance',[4] so a line can be drawn between 'scientific' and 'artistic translation', the latter being 'housed in Applied Linguistics and mainly founded on praxis' (Zuber-Skerritt 1984b: 4). Yet again, in the absence of a consistent theory taking on the performative side of theatre translation, this is viewed in a merely practical way – as shown in the following four pages, which are dedicated to extending Marilyn Gaddis Rose's 1981 six-step strategy for literary translation with two phases that have to do with 'page to stage' transposition.

In this contribution and in the whole collection, the spotlight is still pointed at the translator – who has the impossible task of combining the (ethical and linguistic) demands of his/her art with the requirements of stage production. Thus, Zuber-Skerritt complains that 'the meaning of a play can be distorted and misinterpreted if the translator fails to appropriately transpose the whole network of symbolic signs into the target culture'; on the other hand, she insists that the specialist in drama translation, 'like a theatre critic, has to consider the final production of the play on the stage and the authenticity of the play and its effectiveness on the audience' (Zuber-Skerritt 1984b: 8). The idea that theatre translation should be viewed in performance-centric terms is there *in nuce*, but it is not developed into a full-blown theory: in the end, the reiteration of words like 'problems' and 'difficulties' seems inevitable, as well as the insistence on the fact that '[a] play written for performance must be actable and speakable' (Zuber-Skerritt 1984c: 1).

The problem, as seen above, is one of methodology and theoretical awareness – but it is perhaps also one of technology, as hinted at here and there by Zuber-Skerritt herself. If dramatic writing is to be appreciated in its performative dimension, the 'theatre critic' has to see it presented and acted on stage – more than once, if possible, because 'each theatre performance [...] is different and unique' (Zuber-Skerritt 1984b: 8). The same is obviously true of translated theatre: in order to see how it works, Zuber-Skerritt's 'specialist' would have to watch the target production rather than merely read the target playtext. This, however, would restrict the scope of theatrical translation theory, whose scholars cannot be everywhere at all times – and what is even more problematic is that if a text is relatively stable in time, theatrical productions (as mentioned above) can vary indefinitely. Fortunately, in 1984, film and taping technologies were already available for 'solving the problem of the instability of a performance', as Zuber-Skerritt (1984c: 1) has it in her introduction. Probably, it was also because of newer, even more refined recording technologies that the twenty-first century saw the definitive rise of performance-centric theories.

2.4 From the late 1990s to the new millennium: Performance-centric views, text-centric terminologies

During the course of the following decade, performance- and text-centric views continued to vie for dominance in the field. While Susan Bassnett was certainly influential within general Translation Studies, for instance, she was considered in conjunction with the other scholars of the 'Tel Aviv–Leuven' axis (Gideon Toury, André Lefevere, etc.) rather than as a theatrical translation theorist. Furthermore, as seen above, Bassnett's theories were themselves tentative and 'problematic', an insider's view of how difficult it is to translate a performance-driven work in a world in which most notions of translation are text-centric. In the 1990s, other scholars attempted to define the performative contours of the discipline – but when it came to terminology, they could never bring themselves to get rid of textualism.

Some of these views were shaped by a functionalist approach to translation. In 1997, Sirkku Aaltonen (whose works, some years later, would be instrumental in promoting a performance-centric theory of translation; see §3.1) published an article in which she compared translation to industrial production. While Bassnett's references to *skopos* had been ideologically neutral, Aaltonen's use of Victor Papanek's 'minimal design' model is more consciously political. The theatre translator must not only reflect on the general purpose of his/her work: more actively, he/she must design the work with a thought to 'the social and historical circumstances of its creation' (Aaltonen 1997: 90). It is inevitable, in this context, to consider the realities of stage production among these 'social and historical circumstances'.

More traditionally, other scholars insist on the need for the translated play to contain elements of performability, for the translator to take into account the final destination of his/her work and for a closer collaboration between the professionals of translation and theatre production. Marta Mateo (1997), for instance, observes a series of ways in which performance can influence drama translation, and draws a parallel between the translator working on a playtext and the stage director instructing actors. Mary Snell-Hornby uses the debatable notion of dramatic 'sub-text' to explore possibilities of collaboration between translators, producers and actors (1996), and tries to analyse the (translated) dramatic text in terms of performative potential (1997). The term 'theatrical potential' is at the centre of an article by Sophia Totzeva, who points out the limitations of any text-centric view of drama which does not consider 'nonverbal signals' (Totzeva 1999: 89). And it must also be noted that in this period, theatrical translation historians began to take into account questions of stage production in much more consistent fashion than ever before (see, for instance, Heylen 1993; Leppihalme 2000).

A good illustration of the text-centric elements still present in the most performance-centric of approaches is a collection edited by Carole-Anne Upton in 2000: *Moving Target: Theatre Translation and Cultural Relocation.* Implicit in the title is the assumption that the book deals not just with dramatic translation, but with the transposition of the whole theatrical experience – and that this transposition involves a series of cultural, ever-shifting adjustments (see Maitland 2017). In their introduction, Upton and Terry Hale complain that 'it is still quite common for performance translation to be subsumed within the general category of Literature', and mention as an example Peter Newmark including seven paragraphs on 'Drama' in a twelve-page section on 'Serious Literature and Authoritative Statements' (Hale and Upton 2000: 12). More or less explicitly, the authors draw a correlation between these kinds of statements and the scant consideration given to practitioners:

> The current practice, fairly widespread in Britain at least, of commissioning 'literal' translations to short deadlines and for minimal fees [...] is symptomatic of the low status in which translators have hitherto been held.
>
> (Hale and Upton 2000: 10)

If this lament, as well as the generic acknowledgement that 'A brief survey of theatre history reveals that translation has, at least since the Renaissance, always played a major role' (Hale and Upton 2000: 2), would seem to prepare the ground for a fully performance-centric definition of the field, other passages reveal that Hale and Upton still have text-centric doubts, sometimes even source-bound scruples. They bring up Beckett's 'dogged determination' to control all the aspects of translation and staging as evidence that '[t]he theatre is by definition protean', and that '[i]ts great strength lies in its very anti-literary impermanence' (Hale and Upton 2000: 9). On the other hand, following Venuti, they also worry whether such a version as Addison's *Cato* 'represents an undue betrayal of the source', and waver, in cases of greater 'cultural relocation', between the term 'translation' and alternatives such as 'adaptation' (Hale and Upton 2000: 6).

The same uncertainty of definition can be found in the rest of their collection, whose contributors propose alternative terms such as 'tradaptation' (Cameron 2000), discuss strategies for remaining 'faithful to the spirit and

form' of the original (Johnston 2000) and even present 'cultural relocation'
as a danger to be avoided at all costs (Rozhin 2000). In the absence of an
authoritative theory, the textual source continues to exercise its pull, and all
attempts at studying theatre translation in performance-centric terms are
bound to fail.

Theatre translation: Performance-centric theories in the twenty-first century

Conveniently for summarizing purposes, the new millennium was inaugurated by one of the very few existing monographs on theatrical translation theory, and the first to propose a decidedly performance-centric view of the whole process. §3.1 is entirely dedicated to Sirkku Aaltonen's *Time-Sharing on Stage: Drama Translation in Theatre and Society*, which takes its bearings from Patrice Pavis' notion of 'intercultural theatre' to try and overcome the text-centric bias of former theories. Despite its occasional lapses and uncertainties, this book is the first consistent attempt at considering any target text/performance with some form of 'recognized intertextuality' with its source as a translation, rather than as adaptation or imitation.

This performance-centric tendency is carried forth by two collections of essays and one special issue of *Target*, all published between 2011 and 2013 (§3.2). In the editors' intentions and in a substantial number of contributions, these works attempt to see theatre translation in its totality, comprehending textual transference as well as the interventions of directors, actors, scenographers and all the other agents involved in stage presentation. Again, the influence of Pavis is strongly felt, in itself as well as through Aaltonen's mediation. However, it would be inexact to say that at this time theatrical translation theory became universally performance-centric: as seen in §3.3, text-centric essays continue to be published which maintain the age-old distinction between translation and adaptation, use such outdated concepts as 'faithfulness' and see the whole process in terms of inevitable loss. Significantly, some of these essays are hosted in the performance-centric collections discussed in §3.2, and even Aaltonen (§3.1) is unable to shed the old dichotomies for good.

3.1 Sirkku Aaltonen and the time-sharing of theatre

Sirkku Aaltonen's *Time-Sharing on Stage: Drama Translation in Theatre and Society* (2000) was perhaps the first monograph to organize all past observations on the performative aspects of theatre translation into something approaching a coherent, fully inclusive theory. The inclusiveness of the attempt is reflected in the title and subtitle of the book, which include 'stage' but also 'drama', 'theatre' as well as 'society'. For the first time since Bassnett's early systematic explorations of the field, the viewpoint is not that of the single practitioner: Aaltonen's express purpose is that of viewing the transmission of a theatrical experience as a whole. Also for the first time – though dramatists and their texts are not forgotten – the starting point is not textual, but performative: Aaltonen sees theatrical creations as instances of 'time-sharing' in which everyone, from the costume designer to every single member of the audience, contributes something to the experience (see also Aaltonen 2013).

Though it serves as a presentation of chapter-by-chapter contents, Aaltonen's introduction is far from neutral. The very first page proposes a distinction between the view of translation as striving for a 'mirror-image' of the source and the competing one – familiarized by Lefevere and other Descriptive Translation Studies scholars – according to which any act of rewriting produces 'cultural hybrids'. When the author adds that the 'mirror-image' position makes us feel 'safer' insofar as it 'supports the myth of authenticity', one is left in no doubt as to which of these views is to be preferred (Aaltonen 2000: 1); and if the idea is accepted that translation always creates something new, there is no reason to operate clear-cut distinctions between theatre translations and 'imitations', 'adaptations', 'tradaptations' and the like. Somewhat confusingly on the theoretical plane, Aaltonen maintains part of this terminology – but she hastens to add that imitations and adaptations are still contained within the greater whole of translation:

> The study of strategies employed in theatre translation shows that while some texts follow their sources carefully and translate them in their entirety, others involve degrees of divergence from them through omissions and additions. Theatre translation thus also comprises imitations, which, while openly admitting that they are creating a new play around some idea or concept from the foreign work, still rely on the recognized intertextuality

between the two. Some scholars might want to confine the last two strategies to the sphere of theatre praxis rather than to that of translation, but in this text the decision has been taken to include them, because their exclusion would have left a large and important part of translation work in the theatre outside the analysis. Theatre translation as a genre traditionally employs 'adaptation' (Berman in Brisset, 1996: xvi), which is a 'practice almost as old as the theatre itself' (Harrison, 1998: 10).

(Aaltonen 2000: 4)

The references in Aaltonen's closing sentence have been kept – where they would normally have been substituted by dots within square brackets – because they testify to the author's terminological embarrassment. What the Finnish scholar is attempting to give here is an inclusive definition of theatre translation for any text which displays 'recognized intertextuality' with its source. Since she needs definitions for these kinds of texts – for target texts which have normally been kept out of the range of 'translation proper' – she ends up having recourse to terms like 'imitation' and 'adaptation'. In other words, although she is clearly trying to define theatre translation in performance-centric terms, Aaltonen ends up using the terminology provided by a largely text-centric theoretical tradition. As she herself admits,

The study of translated theatre texts typically draws its material from the text-centred theatre, which is the dominant theatrical form in the Western logocentric tradition.

(Aaltonen 2000: 5)

In order to break, as far as possible, from 'the Western logocentric tradition', Aaltonen crams her book with examples of stage-oriented theatre translation, thus making it clear that text-centric theatre 'is only one form of theatre, although in some traditions its dominance has left all other forms in the shade' (Aaltonen 2000: 17). Her theoretical position has strong roots in the semiotics of theatre, with particular reference to the research of Patrice Pavis. The whole of chapter 1, in fact, is dedicated by Aaltonen to 'Intercultural Theatre', i.e. to all those forms of spectacle which transcend linguistic borders with or without the transmission of texts. The diffusion of Italian *Teatro dell'arte* in Renaissance Europe and Peter Brook's contemporary experiments are different examples of how dramatic practices can travel without the need for textual translation (see also Pavis 2010). In Aaltonen's argumentative network, discussing intercultural theatre well before a section on 'The Exchange of Dramatic Texts' serves the purpose of dispelling the aura of sacredness normally connected with interlingual translations of important plays. It is not by chance that the first textual translations actually discussed are those of Plautus and Terence. Aaltonen is always at pains to underline the fact that even when there is a definite relationship between source and target texts, the latter must not necessarily be seen as subservient to the former.

The third chapter, 'The Time-Sharing of Theatre Texts', is the ideological core of the monograph. Here Aaltonen rejects the categorization of translations as 'free' or 'faithful' (the inverted commas are her own), but at the same time feels that 'different relationships between [source and target] texts must still be accounted for' (Aaltonen 2000: 53). While her case studies span all possible forms of assimilation in the target culture, a rather clear-cut distinction is still drawn between works inspired by 'Reverence' for the foreign and transformations in which the intent of 'Subversion' is more in evidence. When reverence is exercised, translations are mostly text-oriented and plays are viewed as important cultural capital;[1] when the prevailing attitude is subversive, 'rebellion' and 'disregard' are the order of the day, and the focus is more on the target culture and performance. The term 'adaptation' is again employed rather frequently – as a term designating a technique, if not a textual category – and it helps draw a tentative, probabilistic line between textual and performance-driven versions:

> Translation for the stage probably employs adaptation more frequently than does printed literature, and it can be used in theatre translation at times or with texts where it would not be acceptable in the literary system. [...] When the Foreign is not of primary interest in the selection, constraints concerning 'fidelity' to the source text and the invisibility of the translator are not the most important criteria in translation either.
>
> (Aaltonen 2000: 75–6)

Aaltonen's mention of 'the invisibility of the translator' betrays her slight embarrassment with regard to the mainstream of Descriptive Translation Studies, which at the time was still overwhelmingly text-centric. The reference, of course, is to Lawrence Venuti's 1995 *The Translator's Invisibility*. In this monograph, Venuti had convincingly connected the cultural and economic plight of translators in the Anglo-American world (their invisibility) with the request for 'fluent' versions which could be presented as perfect replicas of their originals; to counter this tendency, he had proposed to privilege 'foreignizing' at the expense of 'domesticating' versions. Venuti's idea, in other words, was that target texts had to bear some marks of cultural and linguistic estrangement in order to fight literary imperialism and the marginalization of translators. While Venuti's identification of 'fluency' as a mantra in American translation was accurate, and his ideological position was relevant in the literary world he was describing, his terminology became so popular in the discipline that it ended up being extended to very different contexts. Aaltonen clearly feels that Venuti is a force to be reckoned with, and knows that 'domestication' more or less equals 'evil' in much contemporary discourse of translation; on the other hand, she is aware that in order to describe the actuality of theatre translation, one must avoid making a fetish of 'the Foreign'.

The slight theoretical and terminological uncertainties in *Time-Sharing on Stage* can perhaps be attributed to the text-centric nature of many contemporary discourses on translation, as well as to Aaltonen's partial disconnect from the rest of Translation Studies. Her bibliography is filled with secondary texts on the history and semiotics of theatre, but is relatively poor in terms of updated theories of translation. It is worth noting, in particular, that Gideon Toury is present only with a 1980 article, and that there is no mention of his fundamental 1995 monograph, *Descriptive Translation Studies – and Beyond*. Since Aaltonen frequently uses Even-Zohar's term 'system', it is impossible not to think that complementing that notion with Toury's 'translation norms' would have been instrumental in the attempt at determining how different societies exhibit different priorities for the assimilation of foreign theatre.

3.2 The performance-centric 2010s

As suggested in the previous chapter, the history of theatrical translation theory could partly be read in parallel with the development of video-recording techniques. In the 1980s, it was easy enough to document theatrical performances by means of tape recorders – but the technology, at least at the beginning of the decade, was still relatively expensive, and the tape formats available at the time required considerable storage space. In the following decade, the creation of less cumbersome data storage formats (Video CDs, DVDs) would have made it easier to collect larger corpora of theatrical performances; but the problem of private or institutional storage would still have to be tackled. It was only in the 2000s, and particularly from 2005 onwards (2005 saw the creation of YouTube), that it started to become natural, if not automatic, to think of any kind of public performance as recordable.[2] While in the field of Translation Studies it is always risky to think in terms of technological determinism (Olohan 2017: 265–70; see also Littau 2011), some loose correlation can be observed between these developments and the fact that in the last two decades there has been a marked 'performance-centric turn' in scholarly publishing on theatre translation. Since 2010, in particular, one monographic issue of a specialized journal and two important collections of essays have appeared, all of which can be defined as stage-oriented in their general outlook. While surely the internal history of the discipline has to be taken into account – the progression from Bassnett to Aaltonen, as well as the works setting a precedent in interrogating theatre professionals (Zuber 1980a; Zuber-Skerritt 1984a; Johnston 1996a) – the ready availability of theatrical performances online has inevitably facilitated the formulation of performance-centric theories. It is also noteworthy that translation, both in the form of surtitles for international productions (Marinetti 2013b) and as one of the elements of the dramatic spectacle (Ladouceur 2013; Nolette 2014), is becoming more and more involved in the *performative* aspects of theatre.

The title of *Staging and Performing Translation: Text and Theatre Practice* (2011) leaves the reader in no doubt as to the primacy assigned by its editors to actual stage performances. In their introduction, Roger Baines, Cristina Marinetti and Manuela Perteghella state their intention to focus 'on translation as an empirical process' rather than 'on how translated plays function as cultural products' (Baines, Marinetti and Perteghella 2011: 2). While other collections of essays have attempted to bring together theoreticians and theatre practitioners, they insist, their book 'provides radically new perspectives [...] as it attempts to explore and theorize the relationship between written text and performance starting from actual creative practice' (Baines, Marinetti and Perteghella 2011: 1–2). Though the stated purposes of the collection are more revolutionary than some of its actual contents, the focus on theatrical practice is kept throughout the book, with the inclusion of round tables on collaborative translation (Meth, Mendelsohn and Svendsen 2011), interviews with theatre playwrights/translators (Baines and Perteghella 2011), accounts of 'total', transformative theatre translation experiences (Rose and Marinetti 2011) and generally of essays describing how dramatic translations can be realized with more than an eye to their stage realization (Upton 2011; Baines and Dalmasso 2011). The overall impression is that of 'complex, multifaceted, diverse, cultural and often personal' practices taking precedence over any general theoretical appreciation of what it means to translate for the theatre (Baines, Marinetti and Perteghella 2011: 1). In fact, if there is any general theoretical underpinning to the collection, it resides precisely in this refusal to make practice subservient to theory.[3]

A similar distrust of theory is in evidence in a collection published two years later: *Theatre Translation in Performance*. The editors situate their book within the 'performative turn' lately taken by Theatrical Translation Studies, and identify 'a widespread suspicion about theory' in recent contributions to the field (Bigliazzi, Kofler and Ambrosi 2013: 2–3). This does not mean, however, that there is no theoretical rationale to the collection, or at least to its general introduction: what seems particularly interesting, in this sense, is that Bigliazzi, Kofler and Ambrosi take the premises of the 'performative turn' to their logical conclusions by making the theatre translator a creator in his/ her own right (for similar developments in 'textual' Translation Studies, see Bassnett and Bush 2006; Munday 2007; Masson 2017). If a degree of prudence is still perceptible in their wording, they are upholding the autonomy of target playwrights (as well as highlighting the performative dimension of their work) when they opine that their volume supports 'an idea of the translator as co-subject and co-author of the *performance*, competent *both in textuality and stage-performativity, in verbal and gestic style*, as well as *acting conventions*' (Bigliazzi, Kofler and Ambrosi 2013: 13; italics mine). Again, the rest of the book may not always conform to the theoretical standards set by its editors, containing as it does some practical discussions alongside historical studies provided by scholars working in the fields of theatre, literature and linguistics; but the intentions of the editors are unmistakable, and even if they do not always set the tone, they give a strong colouring to the whole.

Published in the same year and edited by Cristina Marinetti (one of the three editors of *Staging and Performing Translation*), a monographic issue of *Target* on *Translation in the Theatre* is much less coy in its theoretical ambitions. In her introductory article, Marinetti explicitly identifies the lack of a commonly accepted view of theatre translation as a problem for the development of the field. In her opinion, this theoretical uncertainty is due to the liminal position of theatre translation, traditionally squeezed between performance-centric Theatre Studies and text-centric Translation Studies. Given the centrality of 'performativity' in Marinetti's own view, it is not surprising to learn that she envisages Theatrical Translation Studies as an interdiscipline, rather than as a 'subfield of translation studies' (Marinetti 2013a: 309). Following Richard Schechner's vision of theatrical events (or, indeed, of all human events; Schechner 2013; Reynolds 2014) as 'performative rather than representative entities' (Marinetti 2013a: 307), Marinetti duly proceeds to define translation as something that does not (merely) impact on texts, but participates in the transformation of cultural signs that happens on stage. The focus is no longer on how texts are translated and translations are performed, but on how translation participates in the endless iteration-cum-variation of theatrical performance:

> It is useful for our purposes as it allows us to ask different questions that relate not to the extent to which a performance represents a translated text, or a dramatic text is performable, but to the force the text has in performance, what 'it does' and how it functions 'as performance' [...] From this perspective, dramatic texts no longer have meanings to be communicated but 'performative force' [...] that gets transmitted and transformed in a series of 'iterations' [...] or, to use a term that is more familiar to translation studies, rewritings.
>
> (Marinetti 2013a: 311)

In short, Marinetti's theory is that each and every performance is a unique phenomenon brought into existence by a number of agents, including actors, directors, scenographers, producers, the audience and translators.[4] Every performance is, in Austin's (1962) pragmatic terms, a 'performative act'. For translation scholars, what remains to be done is to try to disentangle the illocutionary forces and perlocutionary effects produced by translators – and that is what, much more consistently than in the two previous collections discussed above (see Aaltonen 2013; Hardwick 2013; Johnston 2013), the other contributors to this issue of *Target* set out to do.

3.3 The resistance of the (source) text

A good index of the predominance of performance-centric theories after 2000 is the fact that in this period, even historians of theatre translation begin to give more weight than ever before to matters of staging and performance. Gunilla Anderman, for instance, puts the stage at the centre of her monograph on the English translations of modern European plays (Anderman 2005). Katja Krebs mostly limits the scope of her book *German Drama in English Translation, 1900–1914* to plays which were actually performed in that period (Krebs 2007: 21). In his history of classical Spanish drama in Restoration England, Jorge Braga Riera takes into consideration questions of performance as well as interlingual translation (Braga Riera 2009: 8; see also Heylen 1993; Minutella 2013).[5]

Claiming that all significant contributions after the turn of the millennium are performance-centric, however, would mean creating a false impression. While the above section testifies to the fact that many of the leading scholars are now proposing a view of translation (and translators) as taking part in the process of bringing a target-language production to life, a substantial number of essays and monographs are still being published which focus primarily on the interlingual level of translation. Some of these works, in fact, are included in the very collections of essays and monographic issues which are presented in the section above. Serpieri's contribution to *Theatre Translation in Performance*, for instance, is distinctly source-bound and ultimately text-centric: in his account of a collaboration with Italian director and actor Gabriele Lavia, the Italian critic insists on the 'embedded speakability' of *Hamlet*, requiring 'a faithful response in translation'; and he voices a very traditional, nostalgic view of theatrical transposition when he laments that 'However faithful any translation may try to be to the original text, much is inevitably lost' (Serpieri 2013: 53, 57).[6]

The problem of theoretical inconsistency is a traditional one within the larger discipline of Translation Studies. Every scholar working in the field is able to recollect at least one conference panel at the end of which a member of the audience has offered a question or a comment beginning with the fateful words 'I know nothing about translation theory, but ... '. Translation as a craft or part-time job is practised by many more people than are aware of its workings or its history; even more people have had some experience of trying to convert a string of words in one language into a string of words in another, mentally or in writing. As a result, most academics of all descriptions, and most people in general, feel entitled to their own opinions. As a less embarrassing result, people who have worked as translators for most of their lives sometimes feel that they have a significant contribution to make towards the academic study of translation – and what they end up producing are reinventions of the wheel which are only interesting insofar as they reflect contemporary social norms (see, for instance, Basso 2010; Bocchiola 2015).

A fair example of this strand in Theatrical Translation Studies is provided by Phyllis Zatlin's 2005 *Theatrical Translation and Film Adaptation: A Practitioner's View*. Zatlin is an American academic and theatre translator from Spanish, and her monograph is a precious mine of information on the behaviour of professionals in this field (comprehending as it does interviews with some of the author's colleagues). However, from the theoretical point of view, this book is at least thirty years behind its publication date: very few Translation Studies references are given in general; Toury, Holmes, Lefevere and Hermans are all absent from the bibliography; the main sources of information on the field seem to be Peter Newmark's handbooks[7] and Clifford Landers' old-fashioned 2001 *Literary Translation: A Practical Guide*. Given these theoretical premises, although she proposes a form of theatre translation that is based on 'performability', Zatlin lacks the terminology to articulate her vision. She feels a need to defend translators against 'the old adage, *traduttore, traditore*', but then she seems to rue the fact that in certain cases 'some betrayal is a necessity' (Zatlin 2005: 1). She admits that 'To achieve speakable dialogue, theatrical translators can and do adapt', and then she agonizes for pages on end over the distinction between translation and adaptation (Zatlin 2005: 1, 3, 79; see also Johnston 2011: 13–14). She is, in short, a performance-driven translator who can only articulate her position by means of text-centric, mostly source-bound theories.

Perhaps the full development of a performance-centric theory of theatre translation is impeded by the fact that these forms of text-centric, source-bound resistance are deeply ingrained in the minds of translators and translator-scholars. People who work on foreign texts, after all, normally develop an affection for the words they study or translate, for the language they are written in and for the texts in which those foreign words are to be found. It is therefore inevitable, for many of them, to try and construct visions of translation in which those texts and words are transposed into another language and yet – also – magically preserved. This position is a particularly difficult one to hold in the theatrical field, where texts are normally seen as mere stepladders to the final production: as a result, the scholars who still want to defend the centrality of the text do so tentatively, while admitting that allowances have to be made for the necessities of the stage. The translator, for instance, may be seen as a 'guardian' who has to be aware that 'The transfer of a text via a translation to the stage inevitably involves a series of compromises' (Meech 2011: 136–7); or, conversely, as someone who, while producing 'oven-ready chickens [...] to be cooked and served up by the director and actors to the audience', still has to 'stand up for' the author of the source text (Brodie 2012: 63).[8]

4

Voices from the field of Theatre Studies

In the preceding chapters, and particularly in the sections dedicated to Susan Bassnett (§2.2) and Sirkku Aaltonen (§3.1), references have been made in passing to the impact of contemporary theories of theatre. This chapter expands those references and looks at opinions on translation from within the field of Theatre Studies, as well as at general ideas on theatrical writing and performing which exercise an influence on how theatrical translation scholars view their subject. Specifically, §4.1 focuses on the pragmatic and semiotic approaches that started to hold sway in the 1970s and 1980s, with particular emphasis on the work of Anne Ubersfeld; §4.2 expounds on the notion of 'intercultural theatre' as developed by Patrice Pavis, while §4.3 is more specifically translational, centring as it does on a 2007 monographic issue of the *Theatre Journal* and on other, more recent contributions.

From the perspective of Theatrical Translation Studies, what seems particularly striking here is that although some theories which do not deal specifically with translation have had a far-reaching influence on the ideas of translation scholars, those same theories have not been very influential on views about translation developed *within* the field of Theatre Studies. This is particularly evident in §4.3, where many of the articles under scrutiny display a practical, non-theoretical approach; and it is interesting to note in §4.2 that even Patrice Pavis, when he writes about translation, adopts a slightly more conservative and text-centric viewpoint.

4.1 Pragmatic and semiotic views: Theatre Studies in the 1970s and 1980s

In the first half of the twentieth century, some theatre theorists and practitioners started to question the primacy of language that had been firmly established since Aristotle's *Poetics* (though it had not always been actualized on stage, if one bears in mind such European 'performative' phenomena as Italian *Commedia dell'arte*). Antonin Artaud and Bertolt Brecht, in their different ways, were particularly influential in disrupting the conventions of bourgeois fourth-wall drama: while Artaud called for a 'theatre of cruelty' which would integrate non-Western spectacular forms and foreground lighting, screaming and movement, Brecht insisted on the importance of 'gestus' in informing the demeanour of actors and the events represented on stage (Pavis 2010: 77–93). In both cases, it was self-evidently impossible to think of a playtext that would comprehend all the possibilities to be realized in performance.[1] In these visions of theatre, the directors and performers (not to mention the audience) became at least as important as the dramaturg – and Artaud influenced a generation of avant-garde directors (Peter Brook, Jerzy Grotowski and Eugenio Barba, among others) who acquired the kind of fame formerly reserved for playwrights.

In the academic domain, these developments led a number of scholars, from the 1970s onwards, to try and accommodate the dimension of spectacle into their theories of theatre. One set of strategies for doing this was offered by pragmatics, a relatively new sub-discipline of linguistics that explored the intentional dimension and practical effects of verbal behaviour (Austin 1962) as well as its implicated meanings (Grice 1991: 22–57). As seen above (§2.2), theatre pragmaticians were particularly active in Italy between the late 1970s and the early 1980s: many of their studies concentrated on Shakespeare and the early modern stage – an understandable choice, given that in early modern dialogue performative forces were more often inscribed than explicitly suggested by stage directions (Serpieri 1978; Aston 1983). However, theatre pragmatics in this phase was still fundamentally textual, taking its cue from the play as a repository of performative instructions rather than analysing its actual realization on stage. In its essence and results, this strand of research was not too far removed from the text-bound pragmatic stylistics that was being developed in Britain by the likes of Geoffrey Leech and Mick Short, and whose methods were occasionally being deployed in the analysis of plays as well as novels and poems (see, for instance, Short 1996: 168–254).

A line of scholarly thought that interrogated itself much more consistently on the relationship between page and stage was that of theatre semiotics. Again, the main tradition of twentieth-century semiotics was fundamentally language-inflected (Perron and Debbèche 1999: xiv–xvi), and its first practical applications in the field of aesthetics had concentrated on written literature. One of the first semioticians who tried to adapt this line of thinking to the theatre was the Polish scholar Tadeusz Kowzan, whose monograph on the subject inaugurated the 1970s and was significantly entitled *Literature and Spectacle in Their Aesthetic, Thematic and Semiologic Relationships*. In part, what is meant by 'relationships' here is the fact that plays have often depended on literature as a mine of myths, plots, characters and so on – but Kowzan also tries to identify the differences between written literature and staged spectacle, and does so by distinguishing between spatial arts (painting, sculpture, architecture) and temporal arts (music, literature). Self-evidently, the theatre exists at the intersection of those planes, and therefore a dramatic performance cannot be seen as a mere 'translation' of a play: theatrical events are complex *Gesamtkunstwerke*, where the written words, their interpretation by actors, the actors' physical qualities, the soundtrack and the lighting all contribute to the final effect.

A more explicit judgement on the distance between play and performance is uttered by Anne Ubersfeld, whose 1977 *Lire le théâtre* can be considered as a *summa* of this early phase of semiotic reflection. In her strongly theoretical first chapter, Ubersfeld starts out by debunking the idea that performance is produced by text. In what she calls the 'classical' view of theatre, it is the director's job to translate the play as faithfully as possible into another semiotic system. However, with another revealing borrowing from the terminology of translation theory, the theorist says that it is impossible to identify any 'semantic equivalence' between these two systems, and contrasts this 'classical' vision with the 'rejection' of the text by the avant-garde:

> A first possible way of seeing things is the 'intellectual' or pseudo-intellectual, classical way, which assigns privileged status to the text and views performance as no more than an expression and translation of a literary text. The director's job is to 'translate into another language' ['traduire dans une autre langue' (between inverted commas in the source text)] a text towards which her or his primary duty is to remain 'faithful' ['fidèle' (between inverted commas in the source text)]. This attitude presupposes an underlying basic idea of *semantic equivalence* [*équivalence sémantique*] between the written text and its performance [...]

This equivalence is very likely [risque fort d'être] an illusion. The totality of the visual, auditory, and musical signs created by the director, set designer, musicians, and actors constitutes a meaning (or multiplicity of meanings) that goes beyond the text in its totality [...]

The other approach, one that is much more common in modern or avant-garde theatrical practice, is a sometimes radical rejection of the text [le refus, parfois radical, du texte]. Theatre is seen entirely in the ceremony that takes place before or in the midst of spectators [est tout entière dans la cérémonie qui se réalise en face ou au milieu des spectateurs]. The text is only one among several elements of performance – indeed maybe the least important element [peut-être le moindre].

(Ubersfeld 1996a: 13, 15; Ubersfeld 1999: 5, 6–7)

Though Ubersfeld is simply presenting two opposing views before embarking on her own analysis, her position seems clear. On the one hand, she does not believe in a fully textual vision that sees performance as a 'translation' of text – there are too many things in a theatrical experience which create meanings of their own and cannot be fully predicted or controlled by even the most detailed of plays. On the other, she cannot bring herself to endorse the position of those who, like Artaud or Artaud's most extreme interpreters, would like to completely reject the text as a factor of performance – a 'radical' position which risks producing another 'kind of illusion, inverse and symmetrical' (Ubersfeld 1999: 7). She concludes that dramatic and theatrical signs belong to two disparate orders of semiotics, and that 'It is not possible to use the same tools to examine both textual signs and the non-verbal signs of performance' (Ubersfeld 1999: 7). But if in theory she takes an intermediate position between a textual and a performative semiotics of theatre, in practice she is mostly confined, in the chapters that follow, to the study of playtexts – the verb 'reading' in her title being usually intended in a literal rather than metaphorical sense. Though she ponders questions of theatrical space, and the 'translation' from page to stage, her discussions of character and the actantial model, of theatrical time, discourse and idiolect, are mostly based on texts. This reliance is made even more evident by the choice of playwrights whose work she examines in *Lire le théâtre* and her subsequent monograph, *L'école du spectateur* (Ubersfeld 1996b): Shakespeare, Racine, Molière and Goldoni are much more frequently at the centre of her analysis than Bertolt Brecht.

Although Ubersfeld does not discuss the interlingual transformation of plays and performances, her semiotic vision of theatre has a direct bearing on theatre translation – as do other views predicated on the uneasy relationship between a 'dramatic' and a 'performance text' (Elam 1980: 208–9). Clearly, if this kind of approach is adopted, translating theatre can no longer be seen as a mere interlingual activity – hence Bassnett's focus on the necessities of stage production as a good guide for the theatre translator. On the other hand, the text is not viewed as merely dispensable, and theatre semiotics at this time is still largely a text-centric discipline – hence Bassnett's insistence on the difficulty of translating a play while keeping the stage in mind. In this phase, theatrical performance is seen as a semiotic system in its own right, but a degree of dependence on the playtext is still taken for granted – if nothing else, at least in analytical terms; accordingly, the theatrical translation theorists who use semiotic theory as their starting point are presented with an insoluble conundrum, and end up thinking of the translator as lost in the middle of a labyrinth.

4.2 Patrice Pavis and Intercultural Theatre

In the late 1970s and early 1980s, when Anne Ubersfeld was publishing her monographs *Reading Theatre* and *The School of the Spectator*, another semiotician, Patrice Pavis, was working on the same topics and drawing similar conclusions. His articles from this period hinge on questions such as the difficulty of founding a semiotics of the theatrical gesture (Pavis 2000: 95–125; 167–91), the challenge posed to theatre semiotics by the avant-garde (Pavis 2000: 193–206) and the possibility of defining a *texte spectaculaire* as distinct from the playtext (Pavis 2000: 231–3). Artaud and Brecht are much quoted and commented on, and Ubersfeld's work is occasionally referenced: all in all, Pavis is much less text-centric in his outlook, but his approach is still tentative and largely problematic ('Problèmes d'une sémiologie du geste théâtral'; Pavis 2000: 95).

Things changed between the late 1980s and the early 1990s, when Pavis started to move beyond the page–stage duality ('We are now beyond the quarrel between a semiology of text and a semiology of performance'; Pavis 1992: 2), and towards a definition of what he called 'intercultural theatre'. This notion and its development were influenced by a new wave of avant-garde theatre which saw directors, rather than playwrights or theorists, as the prime movers of innovation. Whole chapters or sections of Pavis' *Theatre at the Crossroads of Culture* are dedicated to complex productions such as Eugenio Barba's *Faust* (1989) and Peter Brook's Indian epic, *Mahabharata* (1986).[2] Having to make sense of these shows sifting Eastern cultures through Western values, or making different performative traditions converge and coalesce, Pavis reacted by proposing a sociosemiotic, 'materialist theory of intercultural appropriation' (Pavis 1992: v). He proposed interculturalism as a sort of updated model of intertextuality, and the only appropriate approach 'to the task of grasping the dialectic of exchanges [...] between cultures' (Pavis 1992: 2).

Again, this (socio)semiotic approach did not directly concern itself with theatre translation, except on specific occasions about which more is said below. It is evident, however, that the idea of theatrical performances representing a locus where different cultures are appropriated, sifted and transformed is germane to the notion of 'cultural translation' (see Maitland 2017), if not of translation *tout court*. The 'hourglass of cultures' used by Pavis as a visual representation of what happens in intercultural theatre could well be adapted to serve as a diagram for theatre translation (Figure 2).

If one substitutes 'translation' for 'adaptation' (3, 4, 7), this figure can serve as a description of what theatre translation does: in the passage from source to target culture, a number of interventions occur which involve all

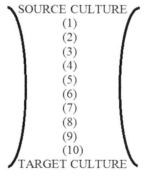

SOURCE CULTURE	
(1)	cultural modelling
(2)	artistic modelling
(3)	perspective of the adapters
(4)	work of adaptation
(5)	preparatory work by actors
(6)	choice of theatrical form
(7)	reception-adapters
(8)	artistic modelling
(9)	sociological modelling
(10)	cultural modelling
TARGET CULTURE	

Figure 2 The hourglass of cultures (adapted from Pavis 1992: 4).

the agents having a say in the transaction, from source/target playwrights and directors (1, 2, 8, 9, 10) to the actors (5) and the audience (7). Sociological, anthropological and cultural constraints apply, which lead to the end product of stage performance. Pavis adds that on the two opposite ends of a filtering spectrum, the hourglass can turn into either a 'mill' (the source culture gets ground into a different powder) or a 'funnel' (the source culture is not sifted at all) – two alternatives which, if the analogy with Translation Studies is maintained, remind one of Venuti's 1995 distinction between 'domesticating' and 'foreignizing' versions. The influence exercised by Pavis on Sirkku Aaltonen's notion of theatrical 'time-sharing' is very evident here: 'intercultural' theatrical productions are not seen as stemming from a single mind, but as the final result of a co-habitation of creative forces. Analogously, theatre translation cannot proceed from the translator alone: too many agents intervene before the end product reaches the stage; and just as Pavis sees intercultural processing on a scale of sifting from 'mill' to 'funnel', so does Aaltonen distinguish between translations inspired by subversive and reverential attitudes (§3.1).

Interestingly, when Pavis busies himself with translation proper, he does not draw the conclusions that his intercultural model would seem to warrant. His chapter 'Toward Specifying Theatre Translation' does indeed state that 'in order to understand the transformation of the dramatic text, written, then translated [...] staged and received [...] we have to reconstruct its journey' (Pavis 1992: 133): but it mostly concentrates on the textual part of that journey, and tries to establish how influential it is on the final staging of the target play.[3] In other words, just as in Bassnett and Zuber, it is once again the plight of the individual dramatic translator that is taken into consideration: unsurprisingly, 'problem' with all its derivative words is repeated seven times, 'difficult' or 'difficulty' are used five times in connection with the translator's position ('Hence the difficulty and relativity of the translator's work'; Pavis 1992: 132), and the whole chapter opens on the familiar complaint that although 'the problems of translation [...] have gained some recognition, the same cannot be said of theatre translation'. Though the chapter was written at a time when Descriptive Translation Studies was beginning to become fashionable, its only translation theory references are to Levý, Mounin and a 1984 article by Snell-Hornby on 'speakability'. It will be left to Aaltonen and to the theorists of the

2010s to work out the full implications of Pavis' notion of intercultural theatre
for theatre translation.

4.3 Between theory and practice: Theatre Studies and translation after the year 2000

The situation outlined in the two sections above has remained more or less
unaltered to the present day: while theatre scholars have produced general
views of stage performance that have influenced Translation Studies, they have
not come up with any definitive, coherent theory of theatre translation. Two
general and concurring tendencies seem to have thwarted developments in
this direction: on the one hand, there has been a reluctance to abandon the
distinction between 'translation' and 'adaptation' and an inability to fix the
boundaries in any universally recognized manner; on the other, many articles
and monographs on theatre translation have been written by translators.[4]
As an example of this double bind and the ensuing theoretical confusion,
one can look at the variety of articles presented in the 2007 special issue on
translation of *Theatre Studies*. Of the four full-length articles included in
the volume, one uses the notion of translation in an extended, metaphorical
sense (Versényi 2007); two look at the dynamics of domestication and
foreignization in Japanese and Chinese Theatre (Curran 2007; Liu 2007); one
is about intersemiotic translation (Bay-Cheng 2007); and one discusses the
ways in which translation is represented on stage (Spencer 2007). The rest of
the issue is occupied by shorter 'forum' articles, mostly written by translators
and dedicated to establishing whether or not one should be 'faithful to the
author's intentions' (Senelick 2007: 372) or if, on the contrary, 'a fully faithful
translation is a utopia' (Spregelburd 2007: 376). As one would expect, references
to Translation Studies are practically non-existent in the forum section and
very general for the longer articles.[5] It is difficult to make theoretical sense of
all this, and the editor, Jean Graham-Jones, does not go beyond some vague
comment to the effect that translation can no longer be viewed as the simple
'"carrying across" from one language to another' that 'the word's etymology
might suggest' (Graham-Jones 2007).

There are, of course, several interesting contributions in this special issue;
and the years after 2007 have seen the publication of brilliant articles and

books on theatre translation from within Theatre Studies. Perhaps the most interesting recent monograph of this sort has been written by David Johnston, an academic, playwright and theatre translator whose many contributions to the field have been quoted in various chapters of this study. His *Translating the Theatre of the Spanish Golden Age* claims to be neither a book of academic criticism nor a work of theatre history, though it has the express purpose of pushing forward 'a dialogue between two worlds that all too rarely speak to each other: the academy and the professional theatre' (Johnston 2015: 1). In order to set up this dialogue, Johnston proposes to analyse his own translations of Spanish *siglo de oro* classics, trying to avoid both conventional breast-beating and 'the drum-banging claims that translators sometimes make for the elegant fidelity of their work' (Johnston 2015: 2). As a professional, Johnston is well aware of two facts: on the one hand, '[t]ranslation is a re-creative art' (Johnston 2015: 2); on the other, theatrical recreation is a collaborative enterprise, forcing the textual translator not only to grapple with the source author but also to join hands with directors and actors.

Johnston is thus perfectly placed to provide insightful descriptions of the problems he was faced with, the source texts on which he worked and their impact on the modern English-speaking stage. What is missing from his monograph – and this is not the author's fault, but an indicator of the state of the art – is a theory of theatre translation that can be taken for granted throughout. The very fact that Johnston feels the need to point out that translation equals recreation, that it can provide no 'transparent window' for the original to shine through (Johnston 2015: 2), is a sign of theoretical uncertainty. He cannot count, for instance, on a fixed distinction between translation and other terms of art, such as adaptation or imitation – a lack that is very significant in a field where translated performances rely on 'literals' which are then modified for the stage (see Brodie 2018a). Of course, the theoretical limitations of Johnston's book are partly a matter of choice, partly a consequence of viewpoint: here as in Bassnett's articles of the 1980s and 1990s, as well as in many recent studies coming from the field of Theatre Studies, the perspective is that of a single translator who, though he successfully avoids the twin pitfalls of apology and self-flagellation, will necessarily find it difficult to view the results of his and his collaborators' work in a completely neutral, product-oriented manner.

Part II

Terms and methodology

Proposing a methodology for the study of theatre translation

This chapter is intended as a bridge between the theoretical and practical parts. §5.1 explains and justifies the use of the term 'theatre translation', reprises some definitions and approaches from Part I and proposes a pragmatic, product-oriented view of each theatre translation as a target theatre act. In §5.2, the traditional distinction between translation and adaptation is consequently abandoned in favour of an all-encompassing view of theatre translation, which is seen as comprehending all kinds of rewriting and refashioning. This view is then further articulated in §5.3 by appropriating and extending Jakobson's 1959 definition: four aspects of theatre translation are envisaged, which cover all features of target theatre acts, from the interlingual recreation of a play to the remodelling of previous performances. Finally, in §5.4 the practical chapters of Part III are presented as illustrations of this model.

5.1 Definition: Theatre translations as theatre acts

At a distance of half a century from the inception of Descriptive Translation Studies, and four decades after Bassnett's early theatrical explorations, the time seems ripe for a comprehensive theoretical definition of the nexus between theatre and translation. As regards the linguistic transposition of text, after all, such comprehensive theories have been circulating since the late 1980s at the very least, with scholars from the fields of linguistics and comparative literature providing complementary visions of what it means to translate and how translations should be judged (Snell-Hornby 1988; Toury 1995). In the theatrical domain, by contrast, as early as 1980, André Lefevere was denouncing the shortcomings of contemporary literary and linguistic approaches to a craft that involves so much more than just one person transferring words from page to page:

> Whether linguistically oriented or not, the study of translated dramatic literature has been treated extremely superficially by translation studies. It is easy to see that a linguistics which had not discovered the central notion of pragmatics could not devote too much energy to one of the most important aspects of drama, whereas literary analyses of translated dramatic texts very often were confined to its textual dimension, to what was on the page. Neither discipline developed the necessary tools to deal with other dimensions in a satisfactory way.
>
> It would seem, for reasons described above, that the study of translated dramatic literature would do well to eschew all normative pretensions. It might productively concentrate on two main fields:
>
> a) The pragmatics of production, in which the way a play is produced can also be seen as a type of text processing, and
>
> b) the way in which certain productions influence the target dramatic literature.
>
> (Lefevere 1980: 160–1)

The terminology in Lefevere's diagnosis now sounds outdated and misleading: he criticizes literary analyses for being too 'confined to [the] textual dimension', yet he himself uses the terms 'dramatic literature' and 'dramatic texts' four times, and seems most preoccupied with the impact theatrical productions have on play-writing traditions. Once these contradictions are factored out, however, Lefevere's suggestions are still valid, and prefigure a lot that has been written since. On the one hand, he proposes using post-Chomskyan, pragmatic linguistics to describe artefacts whose realization owes as much to language as to other sign systems; on the other, less explicitly but no less convincingly, he advocates extending to the translation of theatre the same kind of non-normative analysis reserved by Descriptive Translation Studies for textual translation. The idea seems to be (in [a], for instance) that it is translation products rather than translation processes that should be the focus of research: rather than defining what ought to happen in translation, or which strategies translators ought to adopt, Descriptive Theatrical Translation Studies would busy itself with what was actually produced in a certain place at a certain time.

While a number of descriptive works have appeared in the last few decades, these have mainly focused on the past, and have as an inevitable consequence concentrated on the textual dimension (even when they have insisted on the performative aspects of plays). By contrast, many of the recent monographs discussing theatre translation as a whole, encompassing both 'page' and 'stage', have yet again been written from the point of view of single translators or theatre professionals (see, for instance, Johnston 2015; Brodie 2018a; Jeffs 2018). These studies are full of precious insights as to what actually goes on when translations get written and staged, but they sometimes lack the detachment of the scholar discussing someone else's work. The same considerations apply to Bassnett's 'translator-centred' studies: trapped inside the labyrinth of their own work, analysts are impeded from taking a broader view from above. This centrality of the translator and the translator process is also partly in evidence in the three recent collections discussed in §3.2 (in the single essays, rather than in the books as a whole), and may help explain the reluctance of some editors to theorize about their subject.

As regards the pragmatics of theatre translation, the main studies advocating its development are roughly contemporary with Lefevere's above-quoted article, although more recent articles on the matter have been penned by the same scholars who were working in that direction in the late 1970s and early 1980s, often with the same text- and source-centric bias (see Serpieri 1978, 2002, 2013). From the 1990s onwards, text-centric Translation Studies has seen a small flowering of pragmatic approaches aiming to provide an updated linguistic account of the translational process. Basil Hatim and Ian Mason, for instance, have identified the main illocutionary force deployed by a text as a 'text act' – a concept which can be used to investigate pragmatic changes occurring in the interlingual passage (Hatim and Mason 1990: 78; Hatim 1998). Morini (2013b: 29–45) has extended this notion in order to look at the 'performative functions' displayed by source and target texts in a non-normative, non-source-bound manner.[1] No such neutral and comprehensive terms have been provided by pragmatic studies of theatre translation, which have generally confined themselves to showing how the pragmatic value of certain source wordings can be preserved on the page and/or on stage (see, for instance, Wolf 2011).

This monograph advances a neutral, descriptive and pragmatic view of the process whereby a source theatre act is transformed into a target theatre act. As anticipated in the introduction to this book, it proposes to call this process **theatre translation**. The term is by no means new, and it has gained great currency in the last three decades as a result of a 'performance-centric turn' of theatrical translation theory.[2] Though most scholars who use it have shied away from providing a single concise definition, it has clearly been the label of choice for all those who view the translation of theatre as a complex collaborative job, rather than something that is produced on the page and then gets transferred onto the stage. It reflects an awareness that staging and translating theatre are not only similar tasks but also, quite often, related aspects of the work required to present a show to an audience (Laera 2019: 18–25). Therefore, even on those occasions when it is possible to distinguish between the contributions of different agents, the term will be used to signify the final net result of all the forces intervening in the transposition.

5.2 Negative definition: Theatre translation, not adaptation

A focus on end products should be a given in a discipline holding that translations are 'facts of target cultures' (Toury 1995: 23), but, as said above, the field is still largely dominated by practitioners, and as a rule different kinds of translation have been given different names. A distinction is very often drawn, in particular, between the notions of 'translation' and 'adaptation',[3] even though the confines between the two concepts tend to shift between one study and the next and even, most confusingly, within the space of a single article or monograph. The 2010s, as a matter of fact, have seen a flowering of 'Adaptation Studies', mainly focusing on intersemiotic translations from text to screen, but sometimes involving the field of theatre. The *Journal of Adaptation in Film and Performance*, active since 2007, has hosted a variety of articles highlighting the conflict or agonizing over the distinction (O'Thomas 2013; Connor 2018; Fois 2018). In 2013, Katja Krebs has edited a collection of essays on *Translation and Adaptation in Theatre and Film* that is as interesting as it is terminologically confusing: Krebs herself admits that no fixed boundaries can be established between the two notions (and the related disciplines of Translation and Adaptation Studies; Krebs 2013: 3), as do other scholars contributing theoretical or practical explorations of the field (Cutchins 2013: 59; Minier 2013: 14; Hand 2013: 159). In the end, as Riita Oittinen (2000: 80; quoted by Minier) opined when discussing another genre that is often transformative (the translation of children's literature), 'the main difference between translation and adaptation lies in our attitudes and points of view, not in any concrete difference between the two' (see also Minutella 2013: 39).

Even though 'adaptation' is still a popular term in the world of theatrical production (mainly standing for the process of transforming a text for the stage; Brodie and Cole 2017; Brodie 2018b), it seems much more sensible to avoid its use in Theatrical Translation Studies. After all, as David Johnston put it more than twenty years ago, 'every act of translation is an act of transformation' (Johnston 1996b: 66) – and, one might add, every act of transformation is an act of translation. From the point of view of Theatrical Translation Studies, the fact that the interlingual translation of a play is accompanied by textual adjustments and/or modifications in terms of scene should make no difference at all: the resulting product, the final theatre act, is still a theatre translation.[4] The most plausible reason for the persistence of terms such as 'adaptation' and 'interpretation' is the fact that whereas textual translations, in our post-humanistic world, tend to recreate the *elocutio* but leave the *inventio* and the *dispositio* of the source intact (Morini 2006: 8–11; Robinson 2017: 441), theatre translations often tamper with the plot, the characters, the setting, even the endings of source plays and performances. When certain boundaries are pushed, notwithstanding the more or less universal recognition that the translator is also, at least partly, an author, translators and academics feel uneasy. Yet again, translation scholars might do well to keep in mind that even as far as texts are concerned, the notion of translation as a process that leaves most of the source untouched is relatively new: Geoffrey Chaucer felt no qualms of conscience when he interpolated a translation from Boccaccio with passages from other authors or with lines of his own invention (Chaucer 1988: 574; Bantinaki 2020).

Theatre translation, therefore, is here further defined as the recreation (*any* recreation) of a theatrical event in a different language,[5] whether done with a strong emphasis on text or on performance. This recreation can happen on all textual and performative planes – or, as Jean Graham-Jones (2017) has recently put it, '[t]he act of theatrical translation can take place in front of a computer, in a rehearsal room, in a café, over Skype, and of course in front of an audience'. The inherently collaborative nature of theatre translation (Meth, Mendelsohn and Svendsen 2011; Laera 2011, 2019; Belingard 2017: 497–8; Brodie 2018b; Pfeiffer, Richardson and Wurm 2020) should alert theorists to the fact that in this field, it is often impossible to distinguish between the translator's (or translators') work and the contributions offered by other professionals with any clarity. Even more than in general Translation Studies, therefore, it is analytically sounder to look at finished products, at the evidence provided by the target theatre act.

5.3 The four aspects of theatre translation

Once the idea of theatre translation as turning (a variety of) source theatre acts into target theatre acts is established, a methodology is still needed to distinguish between its various operations. When a Shakespearean play is performed in a non-English-speaking country, for instance, the first step will be to create or procure a working textual translation of the play; almost certainly, that text will then get modified in rehearsal or successive performances; the mise-en-scène will also have a bearing on the effect of the text, and it will inevitably differ from any previous mises-en-scène and be quite distant from Elizabethan staging conventions (unless the production is meant as historically accurate); finally, every successive performance will produce different effects on different audiences at different venues.[6] While looking at the target theatre act resulting from these operations, the analyst will need a terminology to distinguish between these planes.

That terminology – with its accompanying methodology – can be easily obtained by appropriating and extending Roman Jakobson's 1959 tripartite definition.[7] When a translated Shakespearean play is modified for the stage by a theatre company, what happens is that those intralingual tweaks, additions or erasures transform an initial interlingual translation. When the effect of each line is influenced by the mise-en-scène chosen for the production (one need only think of *Richard III* in Nazi garb, but even facial expressions and ironic tones are interpretive), that influence can be viewed as an intersemiotic translation of text into performance. Finally, whenever a Shakespearean production alludes to or modifies one or more previous Shakespearean productions (Carlson 2001), the relationship between mises-en-scène must be described as intrasemiotic (or intersemiotic if, for instance, the previous production is a cinematic one). Thus, as shown in Figure 3, every theatre translation can be seen as having four potential aspects.

This four-way definition includes operations which normally go by some other name in theatre parlance: as seen above, intralingual translation is normally dubbed 'adaptation', and the same label is assigned to productions in which substantial changes are made at the intra-/intersemiotic level; the intersemiotic translation of text into performance is commonly called

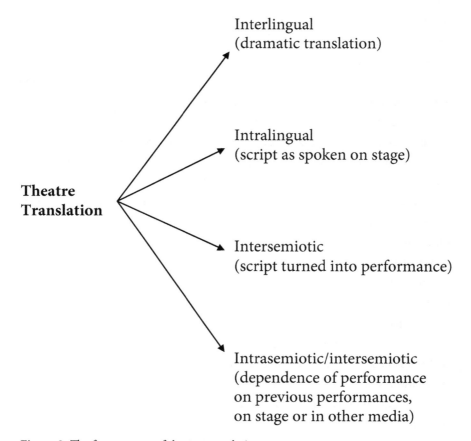

Interlingual
(dramatic translation)

Intralingual
(script as spoken on stage)

**Theatre
Translation**

Intersemiotic
(script turned into performance)

Intrasemiotic/intersemiotic
(dependence of performance
on previous performances,
on stage or in other media)

Figure 3 The four aspects of theatre translation.

'mise-en-scène' or 'production'. The advantage of considering all these operations as pertaining to theatre translation is twofold: on the one hand, as seen above, it eliminates all terminological confusion between translation and other transformative processes; on the other, it dispels the sense of despairing complexity felt by the early theorists. It turns out, after all, that the feeling of being trapped in a labyrinth experienced by the textual translator was only due to the presence of other agents at work on the same process. The end product belongs as much to the textual translator as it does to the directors, the actors and all the other participants in the transaction. In that sense, theatre translation is always, at least potentially, plural and collaborative.

As mentioned above, this idea of theatre translation as a complex, collaborative process of transformation is not new. Pavis' image of the 'hourglass of cultures' represents theatrical performance as a totalizing filtering process, though it does so in cultural terms and avoids making explicit reference to linguistic translation. Aaltonen (2013) has tried to apply Schechner's performance studies and Actor–Network sociology to the field in order to describe the contributions of various kinds of players – human actors and non-human actants – to the process of theatre translation (see also Schechner 2013: 250; Buzelin 2006: 137–41; Bogic 2010: 181–3). Also, the performance-centric collections of essays described in §3.2 are all very eloquent on the contributions of various classes of theatre professionals. While incorporating these findings and insights, the idea of theatre translation as a four-way process leading to a target theatre act is more flexible and product-oriented: in any given act of translation, one, some or all of the operations outlined above can be involved; and whether single human or non-human contributions are traceable or not, their impact is observable in the final theatre act. In being product-oriented, this analytical proposal appears to contradict some of the humanizing, personalizing tendencies which have gained ground within Descriptive Translation Studies in the last decade or so (see, for instance, Chesterman 2009; Pym 2009; Munday 2014; Morini 2020a; or Robinson 1991 as an early step in this direction); but if 'translator-centred translation studies' may be seen as a welcome correction to the objective, generalizing sociological bent of the discipline in its textual incarnation, in the theatrical domain the focus has always tended to be on personal experience, and the objective sociological phase has yet to begin.

5.4 From theory to practice: An outline
of the following chapters

The practical chapters in Part III are conceived of as illustrations of this methodology, as well as of the theories discussed in Part I. Therefore – as seen in the introduction to this book – although Chapter 6 analyses a Renaissance play and Chapter 8 ends with a discussion of a performance that is still touring Europe, the main organizing principle of Part III is not one of historical completeness. No attempt is made to give accounts of theatre translation at all times and in all places, or of the translation of all forms, genres and styles of theatre. Besides the sheer impossibility of providing such an account from the viewpoint of a single scholar, the enterprise would go beyond the scope of this study, whose aim is to summarize all significant historical views on translation and theatre, subsume those views into a single approach and demonstrate its applicability.

The progression of the practical chapters, therefore, corresponds to the articulation of the four aspects of theatre translation outlined in Figure 3. Chapter 6 is about some early modern translations of Giovanni Battista Guarini's pastoral tragicomedy *Il pastor fido*; given the nature of that play and our relative lack of knowledge on its performative history, the focus there is mostly intra- and interlingual, though some intersemiotic speculation is attempted and the written record of one complete theatre translation is examined. In Chapter 7, a couple of recent mises-en-scène of twentieth-century works are analysed which demonstrate that no understanding of target theatre acts is possible without carefully considering questions of dramatic history (intralingual translation, or handing down) and performative tradition (the intra- and intersemiotic fourth level). Finally, Chapter 8 discusses the ways in which all four aspects of theatre translation can be seen to operate in contemporary 'experimental' productions.

While there are no pretensions of universality in Part III as in the rest of the book, it remains to be noted (again, as anticipated in the introduction) that there is a purpose to its chronological arrangement. Chapter 6 shines a light on the period in which European translated plays started to be appreciated as written 'literature' – a development which explains the textual focus of many approaches discussed in Part I and the text-centric bias still shared by many practitioners and audiences. That bias, as will be seen in Chapter 7, leads many productions to hide their practices of indirect translation and intersemiotic derivation. Chapter 8 discusses works which, while not necessarily more recent, are more 'contemporary' than those analysed in Chapter 7, in that they tend to foreground visuals and sound at the expense of language – but as will be seen in §8.4, even these forms of spectacle may be seen to retain some vestigial, post-humanistic reverence for text.

Part III

Practice

Renaissance translation between text and stage: The European circulation of *Il pastor fido*

This chapter explores the dissemination of one work, Giovanni Battista Guarini's pastoral tragicomedy *Il pastor fido*, in the Europe of the late Renaissance – i.e. at a time when theatrical modes, plots and motifs travelled far and wide but printed plays began to be seen as part of what is now called the 'literary canon'. Normally, in this period, theatre texts were published after a successful stage run, but they were translated if they were thought to possess poetic merit (rather than theatrical potential). Predictably enough, most of the existing versions were conceived of as reading material rather than as scripts. Nevertheless, some translations of *Il pastor fido* appear to have been written with an eye to possible performances, at least one printed play was the record of an actual theatre translation, and all versions may have influenced other pastoral plays. Therefore, the plethora of 'faithful shepherds' which appeared in Europe between the end of the sixteenth and the second half of the seventeenth century are sifted not only for their intertextual relationships but also for the traces of performative history they may contain. Though theatre translation and the print medium were becoming separated in early modern Europe, the status of theatrical works was still uncertain enough to allow for different choices on the part of single practitioners.

6.1 Guarini's European fame: A poet, not a playwright

The fame of Guarini's pastoral tragicomedy in verse was established years before it was first published (in late 1589)[1] or staged (probably in 1595 or 1596; Pozzi 2006). Its author began to compose it in 1580, and by 1583 a manuscript version was already circulating and gaining appreciation in the courtly, literary and academic circles of northern Italy (Frodella 2012: 119). The mixed nature and pastoral escapism of the play provoked critical reactions which surely contributed to its notoriety (Bulega 1984), as various failed attempts at staging it at the courts of Mantua, Ferrara, Turin and possibly Rimini may have done (Pozzi 2006: 279). What is certain is that when *Il pastor fido* finally appeared in print and on stage, it was already a prestigious courtly classic: the play was published in Venice by Giovanni Battista Bonfadino, its title page bearing a dedication to the nuptials between Duke Carlo Emanuele I of Savoy and Catalina Micaela of Austria, King Philip II's daughter, whereas the most lavish and best-documented staging of the work took place in Mantua in 1598, during the celebrations following another, even more important European marriage (Sampson 2003).

As illustrated by the genealogical ramifications of its first appearances, *Il pastor fido* was not merely an Italian phenomenon – and in point of fact, European editions started to appear close on the heels of the first Italian book. Just a year and a half later (1591), John Wolfe, printer of Italian books in London, published for Giacomo Castelvetro a volume combining Guarini's play with Tasso's 'pastoral fable', *L'Aminta*.[2] Very few years elapsed before the appearance of versions in all the major European languages, including Latin: the first French translation was published as early as 1593; English and Spanish faithful shepherds followed in 1602; a neo-Latin *Pastor Fidus* in 1604 or 1605; a German *Schäfer* in 1619. The immense popularity of Guarini's masterpiece in the seventeenth century is attested by an enormous number of Italian and translated editions. Also, the continuing influence of the play is evidenced by the striking fact that the existence of one version in a certain language would not hinder other people from creating their own and publishing them – as shown by two more printed translations in English, four more in French and three more in German.

However, before the *Pastor Fido* is hailed as the great theatrical masterpiece of seventeenth-century Europe, a couple of caveats are necessary. As demonstrated by the history of its Italian performances, Guarini's was not the most stageable of plays, because it required (at least in the intentions of its author) a very expensive intersemiotic translation. More generally, this was the time when theatrical writing began to be seen, and translated, as literature: for most people of letters, therefore, it was perfectly possible to appreciate the Italian or translated dialogue on paper without ever hearing it declaimed by actors.

Consequently, while there is a great abundance of textual versions of *Il pastor fido*, the evidence of any mises-en-scène in any language is sparse. As regards Britain, for instance, there are traces of a Latin performance in Cambridge around 1604–5 (Neri 1963: 17), and then nothing until Elkanah Settle's concise theatre translation of the 1670s. By contrast, it can be said that the London book market was almost always provided with at least one version of the play. After Wolfe's above-mentioned Italian edition, a first English translation appeared in 1602 and was then reprinted in 1633. Fourteen years later, in 1647, Richard Fanshawe's much more celebrated translation was printed, and would go on to be re-issued three times before the end of the century. Meanwhile, another translator, Jonathan Sidnam, had decided not to publish his own version because a successful one was already in circulation (Pigman III: 296); Sidnam's text (*c.* 1630) remained in manuscript form, just like the earlier Latin *Pastor Fidus*.

Fanshawe's version is a typical specimen of this textual, 'literary' output. The 1647 *Faithfull Shepherd* turns the Italian *versi sciolti* into very tight iambic pentameter couplets which, as will be seen in the next section, have a lyrical rather than a dramatic force and occasionally elaborate on Guarini's very elaborate elocution. The fact that sometimes, in order to keep faith with his metrical choices, Fanshawe ends up writing unspeakable dialogue in rather convoluted syntax ('Learn women all from me this housewifery, / Make you conserve of Lovers to keep by'; Guarini 1647: 27) demonstrates that what he is interested in is versification rather than dramatic efficiency. This is fully confirmed by the poem 'To the Authour of this Translation', which serves as a preface to the *Faithfull Shepherd* itself – a poem in which John Denham, again in rhyming couplets, famously praises Fanshawe for refusing to follow the 'servile path [...] Of tracing word by word, and line by line' (Guarini 1647: sig. A1r). Denham makes it very clear that the work he is presenting is a poetic, not a theatrical translation: he berates slavish practitioners for producing something that does not bear 'the effects of Poetry, but [the] pains', and exalts Fanshawe because he has managed to recreate Italian 'Numbers' in a different 'Musick' and has spurned 'unhappy Rimes', thus avoiding the most common pitfalls that translating versifiers tend to run into – and rendering Guarini's poetic greatness rather than his words ('They but preserve the Ashes, Thou the Flame'). This is clearly the idea of recreative imitation – also involving a strife with the original, an attempt at outdoing the source author – which was at the heart of post-humanistic, Renaissance views of poetic translation (Morini 2006: 8–17).

An attendant aspect of that idea is that one translates in order to prove one's rhetorical mettle, thus demonstrating one's fitness for courtly office. Guarini himself had completed his play after leaving the Estense court of Ferrara, and one of his purposes had been trying to ingratiate various Italian reigning princes. More than half a century later, Fanshawe prefaced his translation – written and published during the English Civil War – with a royalist dedication of this 'dramatick poem' to young Prince Charles, the future Charles II (Parry 1990: 41–2). Most European translations betray comparable purposes and contain similar dedications – to hereditary princes in the care of the translator-preceptor, as is also the case with Mannlich, the first German translator; to kings and local lords; or to influential ladies who were thought to be the ideal readership for pastoral literature (Caemmerer 2013).

Whatever their individual purposes in publishing their work and presenting it to their patrons, most European translators took it for granted that their 'faithful shepherds' were to be used as reading material rather than as the basis for a future performance. The first French translator, Roland Brisset, explained 'Aux Lecteurs' that he had eliminated Guarini's prologue from his own prose-and-verse rendition because his book was meant 'not for a theatrical performance, but only to be read' ('non pour le representer sur vn theatre, ains pour estre leu seulement'; Guarini 1593: sig. A3r). Thirty years later, Antoine de Giraud presented his own poetic version (mostly in rhyming hexameters) together with a selection of Guarini's and his own poems, and presented his effort to his readers as a poetic one, motivated by the fact that the only version in existence was in prose (Guarini 1623: sig. A5r). Again, the Abbé de la Torche, who produced a third French version, declared that it was more a closet than a stage play ('aussi est-elle plus du Cabinet que du Theatre'; Guarini 1666: sig. A2v). The above-mentioned Mannlich advised his aristocratic charge to treat his German version as a mirror for princes, and his successor Hans Assmann von Abschatz prefaced his own with a single page on poetic translation (Guarini 1672: sig. A3r). Cristóbal Suárez de Figueroa, who bizarrely published two very different translations in 1602 and 1609 (the second one, even more bizarrely, avoiding any recognition of the first), also used his books as presentation copies in the hope of courtly advancement, and composed his 1602 *Pastor Fido*, in particular, as an excuse to try his hand at as many different metrical forms as possible (Guarini 2006–7; see Sánchez García 2019: 191).

6.2 Printed plays in Renaissance Europe, and a few English faithful shepherds

If the inclusion of theatrical writing in the category of literature leads most translators of *Il pastor fido* (or any verse play) to treat it as poetry, in the short run it also seems to have the opposite effect. In early modern Europe, playwrights begin to display the same kind of ambition as their non-theatrical peers – and with the diffusion of print, they are drawn to its promise of permanence and immortality (Andrews 1993: 45; 2014: 125–6). However, once printed plays acquire cultural prestige, theatre translators, too, may be tempted to publish their efforts; and even those whose versions are more poetic than dramatic may wish to replicate some of the stylistic and paratextual features of original printed drama.

The English diffusion of Guarini's play must be seen in the context of these contradictions and this state of flux – and, in fact, the appearance of the earliest editions intersects very interestingly with the history of theatrical publishing. Before 1590, very few stationers, publishers or authors thought it worth their while to print playtexts: bulky romances, collections of stories and historical works were considered to be much more profitable and/or respectable ventures (Straznicky 2012). In the 1590s, however, the plays of Shakespeare and other playwrights began to feature in the catalogues of a few London printers (Schott Syme 2012: 28–9); and by the third decade of the seventeenth century, the notion of the playwright as a great author must no longer have seemed so outlandish, since in 1623 a few former colleagues of the future Bard decided to publish an expensive folio edition of his plays.

The first London editions of *Il pastor fido* appeared between the beginning of the 1590s and the first decade of the seventeenth century, at a time when printing plays was only just beginning to be seen as a viable commercial option. On the face of it, both texts are presented as reading material rather than scripts. The man who prepared and paid for the 1591 *Pastor fido/Aminta* edition, the Italian protestant expatriate Giacomo Castelvetro, dedicated his efforts to Baron Charles Blount because the latter was a known 'lover and ardent follower [...] of our language, and of the writings of its poets' ('amatrice & ardente seguitatrice [...] della nostra fauella, & de gli scritti de suoi poeti'; Guarini and Tasso 1591: sig. A3r). No reference was made in Castelvetro's dedication to the possibility of a mise-en-scène – and again, it is worth remembering that at this point Guarini's play had not yet been performed in Italy or elsewhere. The book is presented as a reprint, made necessary by the fact that it is very hard to find copies of the Venetian edition in England, and its assemblage is clearly the work of a man who hopes to find prestigious employment as a teacher of Italian (the following year, Castelvetro entered the service of James VI of Scotland, later James I of England; see Butler 1950).

Very similar assumptions and motivations seem to underlie the first English version of the play, *Il Pastor Fido: Or The Faithfull Shepheard*, printed 'for Simon Waterson' in 1602. The man who penned this English *Shepheard* has been identified as a Tailboys Dymock, because of a brief dedication to Sir Edward Dymock – Queen Elizabeth's Champion – in which Waterson declares that the translator is recently deceased and the dedicatee's kin (Donno 1993: xxii–xiv; Morini 2021). Apart from this single paragraph signed by Waterson, the short paratext only includes two sonnets – one by the translator himself and one by Samuel Daniel, Italianate poet, playwright and historian. In his poem, Daniel mentions the fact that he has been to Italy with Edward Dymock (see Schlueter 2012). The Queen's champion will surely appreciate the fact that Guarini can now 'Speake as good English as Italian' (a commonplace metaphor in Renaissance translation discourse; see Hermans 1985; Morini 2006: 35–61) – not because Dymock is unable to read Italian, but because this translation demonstrates that English, too, can be poetically 'good', that it can be used to produce a work of art in verse. That this is the main raison d'être of the book (from Samuel's point of view) becomes evident in the last six lines of the sonnet, where the poet recollects past arguments that he and Dymock had with the great Guarini himself, back in Italy. Apparently the Italian poet had sounded less than enthusiastic about the rhetorical qualities of English. Now, in 1602, the very existence of this northern faithful shepherd proves him wrong:

Though I remember he hath oft imbas'd
Unto vs both, the vertues of the North,
Saying, our costes were with no measures grac'd,
Nor barbarous tongues could any verse bring forth.
I would he sawe his owne, or knew our store,
Whose spirits can yeeld as much, and if not more.

           (Guarini 1602: sig. B1v)

Again, these lines present the *Pastor Fido: Or The Faithfull Shepheard* as the kind of imitative translation that attempts to vie with and surpass the original as a poetic work. If in part the competition is between Italian and English,[3] it is obviously the task of the translator to make the most of the linguistic means at his disposal, thus producing a comparable masterpiece. In short, here, as in most prefatory materials of the Guarini editions cramming the book markets of sixteenth- and seventeenth-century Europe, the translator's work is presented as poetry rather than theatrical discourse.

  Other features of this edition, however, point to the possibility that the translator himself and the other originators of the book (i.e. Waterson, presumably Daniel, maybe Edward Dymock) did have some aspects of theatrical discourse in mind. Over the last four centuries, Tailboys Dymock has been accused of incompetence and of excessive adherence to the source text (for a recent summation and reprise of this criticism, see Pigman III 2010: 296); but if the first accusation is partly justified by passages in which he appears to misunderstand the Italian, the second one is easily disproved by pointing out all the scenes in which he cuts Guarini's rhetorical flourishes short and ends up producing something which is not only simpler but also more speakable than his Italian source. Here, for instance, is a passage from the very first scene of the play in which the old Linco scolds Silvio for attending to the excitements of the hunt, rather than giving himself up to the pleasures of love:

Lin. *O Siluio Siluio, a che ti diè natura*	Lin. O *Siluio,*
Ne piu begli anni tuoi	Did nature on these youthfull yeares of
Fior di belta si delicato, e vago	thine
Se tu se tanto a calpestarlo pronto?	Bestow such beautie to be cast away?
Che s'auess'io cotesta tua si bella	Had I but such a ruddie cheeke? so fresh?
E si fiorita guancia;	Farwell to woods, I'ld follow other sports:
	I'ld weare my dayes in mirth: all sommer
	tide

A Dio selue direi;	In daintie shades, winter by the fire side.
E seguendo altre fere	*Sil.* Thy counsell (*Linco*) is like vnto thy
E la vita posando in festa, e'n gioco	selfe.
Farei la state a l'ombra, e 'l verno al foco.	*Lin.* At other pleasures would I aime, were
Sil. Cosi fatti consigli	I *Siluio.*
Non mi desti mai piu, come se hora	*Sil.* So would I, were I *Linco*, but I *Siluio* am,
Tanto da te diverso?	Therefore I *Siluioes* deeds do like, not
Lin. Altri tempi, altre cure,	*Lincoes.*
Cosi certo farei, se Siluio fussi,	(Guarini 1602: sig. B2r)
Sil. Ed io se fussi Linco,	
Ma perche Siluio sono	
Oprar da Siluio e non da Linco i' voglio.	
(Guarini and Tasso 1591: 2–3)	

It is immediately apparent that the guiding principle of Dymock's translation is condensation – his version of this exchange is made up of 11 lines vs Guarini's 18, 85 words vs 106 and 102 syllables versus 162. If this is partly caused by the difference between polysyllabic Italian and monosyllable-rich English, it must be pointed out that in this period elegance and rhetorical *copia* are more or less synonymous, and translators tend as a consequence to amplify, rather than reduce (Morini 2006: 66). Furthermore, a closer reading serves to identify the passages in which Dymock's abridgements are discursive and rhetorical as well as numerical: Silvio's comment on Linco's advice, for instance, is both shortened and simplified ('Thy counsel (*Linco*) is like vnto thy selfe'); Guarini's flowery metaphor ('*E sì fiorita guancia*'; 'such a flowery cheek') is left out altogether; and the proverbial 'altri tempi, altre cure' ('with changing times come changing thoughts') is cut as well. All in all, while the Italian characters sound like courtiers elaborating on long-worn Petrarchan figures, their English counterparts engage in quick repartees which would not sound entirely out of place on the Elizabethan stage ('At other pleasures would I aime, were I *Siluio* / So would I, were I *Linco*, but I *Siluio* am').

One reason why the reader of early modern plays feels that Dymock's translation has theatrical potential is that the kinsman of the Queen's champion has chosen to employ (predominantly, though not exclusively) blank verse – a very far proposition from Guarini's alternate seven- and eleven-syllable lines rhyming freely, and a form which inevitably evokes the contemporary professionals writing for the London public stage. Dymock's pentameter line is often rather irregular, but can sometimes achieve a quality of dignified compactness (particularly when it is *not* irregular: 'Farwell to woods, I'ld follow other sports'). Quite apart from any considerations of aesthetic value, the very use of blank verse, coupled with Dymock's condensing technique, makes the 1602 *Faithfull Shepheard* more theatrical than its Italian source text.

There is no way of knowing whether this effect was intended or created unwittingly by the translator: the only other text we have by him – apart from a 1599 verse satire called *Caltha Poetarum: or, The Bumble Bee* – is the introductory sonnet to this play, in which he uses the familiar self-apologetic argument that it is easier to pursue one's own inventive path than to follow another author's footsteps ('it's harder to reform a frame / Than for to build from groundworke of ones wit'), and declares, again in thoroughly traditional terms, that he has made Guarini an 'English denizen' and fashioned for him, or for his shepherd, a 'sute / of English clothes' (Guarini 1602: sig. B1v). The latter metaphor is too well worn to justify the hypothesis that it signifies the intralingual adjustments attendant on the intersemiotic page-to-stage translation.

That those 'clothes' may also have been intended as theatrical costumes, however – or that their theatrical qualities were noted post-factum by the publisher and/or originators of the work – is shown by the material shape that was chosen for the book containing the first English *Pastor fido*. It has been mentioned above that during the 1590s, a greater number of plays had been printed in London than ever before. A few stationers in particular had been responsible for most of this output, which had consisted of slim quartos parading the name of the theatrical company responsible for the staging in their title pages, maybe as well as the theatre where the play had been or continued to be performed and sometimes, but not always, the name of the author. One of these printers was Thomas Creede, the title page for whose 1599 quarto edition of *The most excellent and lamentable Tragedie, of Romeo and Iuliet* is here reproduced as Figure 4. The play, in this case, is anonymous: it is simply presented as a new revised edition of a text that 'hath bene sundry times publiquely acted, by [...] the Lord Chamberlaine his Seruants'. Below this piece of theatrical advertising stands the emblem of the printer – the crowned, naked figure of truth scourged by a hand emerging from the clouds and surrounded by a motto reading 'Virescit Vulnere Veritas' ('Truth flourishes through injury'; Cary 1994: 45) – and beneath that appear the names of Creede

THE
MOST EX=
cellent and lamentable
Tragedie, of Romeo
and *Iuliet*.

Newly corrected, augmented, and
amended:

As it hath bene sundry times publiquely acted, by the
right Honourable the Lord Chamberlaine
his Seruants.

LONDON
Printed by Thomas Creede, for Cuthbert Burby, and are to
be sold at his shop neare the Exchange.
1599.

Figure 4 The 1599 edition of *Romeo and Juliet*. Folger Shakespeare Library, STC 22323.

himself and Cuthbert Burby, another important publisher of plays who, in this case, presumably paid for the book or shared the costs with him ('Printed by Thomas Creede, for Cuthbert Burby'; Schott Syme 2012: 37).

Since Creede, alongside Burby and a few others, was directly responsible for printing most playbooks between the end of the sixteenth and the beginning of the seventeenth century, and since Creede himself had published or printed more of them than any other stationer between 1590 and 1604 (Schott Syme 2012: 28), it is interesting to learn that the first English *Pastor fido* came out of his printing press in 1602. If I say 'learn' and use the impersonal expression 'came out of his printing press', it is because Creede's name is not in evidence on the title page of this edition. As seen above, *Il Pastor Fido: Or The Faithfull Shepheard* is merely presented as 'Translated out of Italian into *English*', and as having been 'Printed for Simon Waterson' in London, in 1602. The 'Virescit Vulnere Veritas' emblem, however, still stands between the long title and the place of publication. The correlation between this book and its printer is unambiguously established – but the stationer, like the author of the translation (or, for that matter and as regards the title page alone, the source author), remains anonymous.

The reason for this choice can only have been financial: Creede was among a restricted group of investors who had begun to think that the products of the London theatres had some commercial potential in them as books as well as performances. Probably, in this case, he reckoned that the textual translation of an Italian play, however famous its author might be, would not hold the same appeal for theatregoers. Conversely, though, one must think of the motivations of Waterson, and maybe Samuel Daniel (with Edward Dymock as a financial backer?), for choosing Thomas Creede as a printer – for choose him they surely did, given that the stationer did not pay, either in full or in part, for this edition. Whatever their hopes for this work or the commercial/interpersonal uses they intended to put it to – and whether they exhorted Tailboys Dymock to produce a more theatrical version of Guarini or recognized its stage potential when the version was complete – it is evident that they wished to align the 1602 *Faithfull Shepheard* with the popular English dramatic writing of its day. They settled on the kind of slim quarto format in which some of Shakespeare's plays had already been published; they decided to skip Guarini's argument and lengthy courtly prologue in order to cut swiftly to the list of dramatis personae and the beginning of dialogue; and they used the stationer who, in the preceding decade, had printed more plays than anybody else.

The theatrical qualities of the 1602 version stand out even more clearly if this book and this translation are compared with Fanshawe's 1647 royalist edition. The printer of this version, Robert Raworth, also employed the quarto format, but the similarities between the 1602 and 1647 books end there. Even the briefest of scans suffices to establish that the later edition is a much more elegant volume, running to more than 200 pages (whereas around 120 had been enough for the Dymock translation) and decorated with one illustration per act, where the earlier edition had been printed with no image at all apart from the printer's emblem. Various paratextual elements contribute to identifying Fanshawe's version as a poetic work rather than as a translation for the theatre: firstly, the title page presents the book as 'A Pastorall' (not a pastoral play or a pastoral tragicomedy), and is printed to the right of a portrait of the source author bearing no indication that Guarini was a playwright ('Not Mars' is this, but learn'd Apollo's knight: / Of Italie the glory, and delight'); secondly, the translation itself is followed by two poems dedicated to young Prince Charles, the future Charles II, 'At his going into the West' (1645) and 'In the the [*sic*] West' (Guarini 1647: 217, 219). These are royalist Civil War poems in rhyming couplets which hail the prince as 'The hoped cure of our great flux of blood' (Guarini 1647: 219). More interestingly for the present purposes, the poems are said to be 'presented' to the prince, and the first one, in particular, looks like a 'presentation poem' affixed to the Guarini translation, which is offered to the prince 'Together with *Cesar's Commentaries*'. The book itself, in short, is a presentation copy to a royal patron, and as such an assay of the translator's poetic and rhetorical abilities rather than an attempt at creating a stageable text. This hypothesis is further confirmed by the 1664 reprint of this version: seventeen years, a lifetime of strife and a Restoration later, 'divers other poems' by the translator have been added, as well as 'a short Discourse of the long Civil Warres of Rome' (Guarini 1664).

The translation itself is clearly textual and poetic. Famously prefaced, as said above, by the commendatory poem in which John Denham berates previous translators for sticking to Guarini's letter, this English version actually follows the Italian rather closely. It reproduces all the source lines – though in rhyming couplets – keeps the argument and prologue, and uses the choruses as occasions to vie with the original author in rhetorical invention.[4] The passage of the first

Lin. *O Siluio Siluio, a che ti diè natura*	Lin. *O Silvio, Silvio,*
Ne piu begli anni tuoi	Why did frank Nature upon thee bestow
Fior di belta si delicato, e vago	Blossoms of Beauty in thy prime, so sweet
Se tu se tanto a calpestarlo pronto?	And fair, for thee to trample under feet?
Che s'auess'io cotesta tua si bella	Had I thy fresh and blooming cheek, Adieu
E si fiorita guancia;	I'ld say to beasts, and nobler game pursue.
A Dio selue direi;	The Summer I would spend in feasts and
E seguendo altre fere	mirth
E la vita posando in festa, e'n gioco	In the cool shade, the Winter by the
Farei la state a l'ombra, e 'l verno al foco.	hearth.
Sil. *Cosi fatti consigli*	Sil. How's this? Thou art not *Linco* sure;
Non mi desti mai più, come se hora	for he
Tanto da te diverso?	Such counsell never us'd to give to me.
Lin. *Altri tempi, altre cure,*	Lin. Counsell must change as the
Cosi certo farei, se Siluio fussi,	occasion doth:
Sil. *Ed io se fussi Linco,*	If I were *Silvio*, so I'ld do insooth.
Ma perche Siluio sono	Sil. And I, if I were *Linco* would do so,
Oprar da Siluio e non da Linco i' voglio.	But as I am, I'll do like *Silvio*.
(Guarini and Tasso 1591: 2–3)	(Guarini 1647: 8)

scene quoted above for Dymock, again, is a perfect illustration of Fanshawe's aims and strategies:

As in the 1602 version, the English translator needs fewer lines than the Italian writer – but in this case the impression of shortness turns out to be an illusion conjured up by the disparity of metre, for in terms of words, Fanshawe's passage (113) is actually longer than Guarini's (106). That there is no striving towards concision here is also evident in rhetorical and discursive terms. On the elocutionary plane, Fanshawe reproduces all the Italian figures, taking care, for instance, to follow the evolution of the flowery metaphor in Linco's appeal to Silvio's feelings ('Blossoms of Beauty in thy prime [...] fresh and blooming cheek'). On the argumentative plane, the English Silvio follows his Italian counterpart in wondering why Linco has strayed so much from his customary self in giving such advice ('*Cosi fatti consigli* [...] *diverso?*'; 'Thou art not *Linco*, sure; for he / Such counsel never us'd to give to me'); and the English Linco equally responds by saying that with different times come different cares ('Counsell must change as the occasion doth'). All in all, Fanshawe's version is a much better crib for the Italian play than Dymock's.

Fanshawe's 'dramatic poem' was so far from being performable that in 1677, eleven years after the translator's death but just one year after the third impression of his Guarini, Elkanah Settle published a condensed intralingual translation. Settle was a relatively new figure – a professional poet and playwright with no personal fortune and no family connections who had to make his way in the world by sheer force of wit and will (he briefly threatened Dryden's theatrical popularity in the 1670s, and was therefore lampooned in both *Absalom and Achitophel* and *The Dunciad*). Though, of course, the very idea of printing a play involved a degree of pretension to literary greatness (as well as the hope of commercial success and/or advancement), Settle's *Pastor fido: Or, the Faithful Shepherd* is clearly presented as a theatrical rather than as a poetic work. The title page does feature a condensed quotation from Virgil's *Eclogues*, but also the specification that this is an impression of the text 'As it is Acted at the Duke's Theatre'. This page as well as the rest of the book – again, in the quarto format – is completely unadorned, as is proper for the published version of a theatre translation. In his dedication to Lady Elizabeth Delaval, Settle apologizes in advance for having made rather free with Guarini's 'Poem'; but says that he did so because plays are more subject to fashion than any other work of the imagination, and because the source text had some serious theatrical flaws that needed correcting:

> If I am Censured by the Admirers of *Pastor Fido* for being so bold with so received a Poem, I only make this Apology, that *Plays* are strictly tyed up to Fashion, that like costly Habits, they are not Beautiful without it. I confess I have taken a great deal of Liberty in the characters of *Silvano* and *Corisca*, because they were not kept up in the Author: The first of which, in the Translated *Pastor Fido* (for I am a Stranger to the Italian) flag'd in the second Act, and was wholly lost in the two last.
>
> (Guarini 1677: sig. A2v)

There is a fascinating mixture of literary and theatrical discourses here: on the one hand, Guarini is clearly recognized as belonging to a restricted circle of great writers, of the poets which will in time be called canonical (his poem is 'received'); on the other, the Italian author is said to have committed a number of faults which are not permissible on the stage of the 1670s, and which must consequently be corrected. Interestingly, in the theatrical prologue added by Settle himself and addressed to the 'gallants' making up his audience, the playwright refers to Guarini's 'sacred Dust' – a deft, oblique reference to Denham's metaphorical use of 'Ashes' and 'Flame' which characterizes the Italian poet as rather old-fashioned, as well as canonical and long dead (Guarini 1677: sig. A3r). It is to be noted, in this connection, that Settle openly admits that his version of *Il pastor fido* is actually an intralingual translation of Fanshawe's *Faithfull Shepheard*. His play must be ranked with all the purged and simplified versions of Shakespeare that Dryden, William Davenant and others had been creating since 1660. If Shakespeare was perceived as being too long-winded and convoluted (as well as too violent and vulgar; Morini 2007) for a Restoration audience, it is no wonder that Fanshawe got shortened as much as it did by Settle's theatrical scissors:[5]

> *Lynco.* Oh *Silvio*,
> Had I thy fresh and blooming Cheek, adieu
> I'de say to Beasts, and nobler Game pursue.
> *Silv.* A Game more noble? what more Sacred task,
> Could Fortune grant, or his Ambition ask,
> Who for his Country does with Monsters fight [...]

> (Guarini 1677: 1)

Apart from Linco's second and third lines, which are preserved intact from Fanshawe's version, the rest of the passage – evidently deemed superfluous to the development of character or plot – disappears. The 'blooming Cheek' remains, but no further metaphorical mention of flowers and flowering is made. On the argumentative plane, most of Silvio and Linco's sparring and counter-sparring has also been edited out: Silvio simply rephrases Linco's oblique reference to 'nobler Game' by formulating a rhetorical question and implicitly changing the meaning of 'Game' from 'hunting quarry' to 'play'.

6.3 Conclusion: Theatre translations do not make it into print

Settle's *Faithful Shepherd* is a unique document in the European diffusion of Guarini's *Il Pastor fido*, and a rare find in the history of printing. It is the textual record of a theatre translation rather than a literary or poetic version of a famed foreign play. As seen in Chapter 1, with the continental rise of humanistic ideas, translation theory became heavily text-centric. As a consequence, whenever a theatrical work became canonized, it got translated as literature, with all the strictures that entails. Fanshawe's recreation of Guarini, like most European recreations, keeps faith with the source in all its parts and rhetorical qualities; and even the Dymock version of 1602, although it appears to imitate the stylistic and paratextual features of contemporary English drama, must be seen as a literary rather than a theatrical work.

The scarcity of printed accounts of theatre translations, however, does not mean that foreign theatre did not circulate freely on European stages. Even if the scope of the enquiry is confined to England and Guarini's *Pastor fido*, the catalogue of borrowings, rewritings, revisions and influences is enormous. Samuel Daniel, who in 1602 defended the northern virtues of Dymock's version, went on to write a pastoral play, *The Queenes Arcadia*, which was 'presented to her Maiestie and her Ladies, by the Vniuersitie of Oxford in Christ Church' in 1605. The dramatist John Fletcher inaugurated his stage career around 1608–9 with a *Faithfull Shepheardesse* which was received very coldly by its London audiences (Fletcher 1609: sig. A2v; Bliss 1983). And if Fletcher's account tells us that the refinements and complications of the genre did not always resonate on the English stage, that did not keep his peers from importing tragicomic and/or pastoral elements from Guarini and/or his English followers, as attested by the long debate on the direct or mediated influence the Italian playwright had on Shakespeare (Gillespie 2004). In short, the mechanics of European theatrical diffusion is based not on something as simple and relatively unambiguous as the printed translation of foreign plays, but on the circulation of largely irretrievable ideas, motifs and (slightly more retrievable) chunks of text – a situation which has led historians of theatre and theatre transmission to use such capacious concepts as that of the 'theatergram' (Clubb 1989). In terms of the definition proposed in this book, theatre translation happens everywhere and in myriad ways: but since it rarely makes it into print, it is very difficult to follow its history.

This separation of theatre translation from dramatic literature coincided with the gradual acceptance of the fact that playwrights are legitimate writers. As seen above, the publication of the First Folio in 1623 marks the beginning of Shakespeare's canonization. That process arguably took some more decades in England, and centuries in the rest of Europe: but when Shakespeare became the Bard, his writings came to be endowed with the same aura of textual sacredness as other, non-theatrical works. In time, this meant that theatre translation was definitively subsumed into the category of literary translation – an inclusion which ended up making such publications as Settle's *Faithful Shepherd* unacceptable. This situation has endured up to the present day: even in the YouTube age, when it is very easy to find recordings of theatre translations, translated plays continue to be produced almost exclusively in text-centric ways. And if in the case of Shakespeare this separation produces a measurable gap between theatre and printed translations, the next chapter will show that a text-centric bias can remain in place even when the author is not canonized and no translated play is available with which the theatre translation could be unfavourably compared.

Contemporary theatre translation and the persistence of textual bias

Chapter 6 observed the European diffusion of a pastoral tragicomedy in the early modern period, when playwrights were only just beginning to be recognized as proper writers. In the centuries that followed, the inclusion of theatrical writing within the domain of literature brought about a definitive separation between textual versions (the target play being destined for the publishing market) and theatre translations (the source play/performance being brought onto the target stage, but not necessarily becoming a book). That separation is still with us, and its theoretical consequences were explored in Part I. In this chapter, two contemporary Italian productions that illustrate its repercussions on practice are analysed. Neither William Douglas Home's *The Secretary Bird* (§7.2) nor Warren Adler's *The War of the Roses* (§7.3) can be said to be classics of contemporary theatre: their relatively low canonical status, therefore, makes it easier for their Italian producers to use various intermediate sources and to act very freely at all four levels of theatre translation. All the same, because of the norms that are held to apply in (textual) translation, these producers are either silent on their processes of inter- and intralingual, inter- and intrasemiotic translation, or they try to demonstrate the direct dependence of their target theatre acts on a single original textual source.

7.1 The single-source norm and theatre translation

In seven decades of academic reflection on textual translation, a wide variety of hypotheses have been formulated as to what it is exactly that gets transferred in the interlingual passage, and through what kinds of process. For the early 'translation scientists' of the 1950s and the 1960s, it was the meaning or 'significance' of a source text that had to be relayed, with no appreciable modifications (Oettinger 1960: 104). For the German scholars who developed a 'functionalist' approach between the late 1960s and the mid-1980s, it was the main function of the source that was to be transposed in the target text, or the *skopos* of the target that directed which features of the source were worth recreating (Reiss 1969; Reiss and Vermeer 1991: 100). For the exponents of Descriptive Translation Studies, from the late 1970s onwards, every translation was, 'of course, a rewriting of an original text', reflecting 'a certain ideology and a poetics' (Bassnett and Lefevere 1990: Preface) – and it was in accordance with that ideology and poetics that the translator-as-manipulator would produce a 'refraction' of the source text in the target language (Lefevere 2000).

While these are very disparate theories, formulated from contrasting ideological positions and/or different vantage points, there is at least one element that unites them all: in none of them is the possibility entertained that the raw material of translation may not be a single, identifiable source text, written in a single and identifiable source language. Much as ideas on what actually happens in the process have varied, there has been near-universal consensus on this point: the translator works on a source text written in a certain language and reproduces, recreates or rewrites it in another language. One of the few scholars who have refused to accept this as a given is Gideon Toury, who included a series of considerations on 'directness of translation' in his discussion of 'preliminary' norms:

> Considerations concerning *directness of translation* involve the threshold of tolerance for translating from languages other than the ultimate source language: is indirect translation permitted at all? In translating from what source languages/text-types/periods (etc.) is it permitted/prohibited/tolerated/preferred? What are the permitted/prohibited/tolerated/preferred languages? Is there a tendency/obligation to mark a translated work as having been mediated or is this fact ignored/camouflaged/denied?
>
> (Toury 1995: 58; see also 129–46)

Notwithstanding Toury's evident attempt to include all possibilities in his scientific description, the negative language he uses reflects the fact that in contemporary Western societies, indirect translation is generally held in bad repute. And in fact, a recent spate of articles and collections on the subject acknowledge that while this practice is 'alive and kicking in today's society' (Pięta 2019: 6), it is generally considered to be worse than direct translation because of its doubly derivative nature (Assis Rosa, Pięta and Bueno Maia 2017: 114). Again, this is a consequence of the text-centric bias of contemporary Western societies: if the revered 'original' is kept at more than one remove from final users, they will feel that they have no real access to its significance or meaning.

Quite predictably, theatre translation finds itself in a difficult position with regard to the single-source norm. On the one hand, from the Roman Republic to the twenty-first century, theatre companies and authors have made use of whatever texts, modes or scenes they have been able to lay their hands on, with a strong emphasis on performative efficacy. On the other, since humanism, they have had to reckon with the fact that freedom in the use of sources is generally frowned upon as a bad cultural habit. Producers, above all in the domain of popular theatre, will be most interested in drawing big audiences; but producers also live in the culture, and know instinctively that the non-philological handling of sources must either be kept hidden or denied (unless it is embraced – but then the target theatre act is called an 'adaptation'). The next two sections will discuss two recent Italian productions which use a variety of intertextual, intratextual, intersemiotic and intrasemiotic sources, but whose agents still claim or suggest they have taken their bearings from a single identifiable text.

7.2 *Indirect translation and intersemiotic interference:* L'anatra all'arancia/Le Canard à l'orange/The Secretary Bird

Between 2016 and 2018, a company toured Italy with a play called *L'anatra all'arancia* (The duck à l'orange). Its director was Luca Barbareschi, who also played the part of the male protagonist – Gilberto Ferrari, a successful TV presenter whose wife, Lisa, has an affair with a Russian aristocrat. Though the setting was Italian, the playbills presented the performance as directly dependent on the 'text' of William Douglas Home's *The Secretary Bird* ('dal testo The Secretary Bird di W. Douglas Home').[1] Douglas Home was a Scottish author of aristocratic birth who set most of his plays in upper-class society, and whose works were moderately successful in Britain until the late 1960s and largely forgotten after the 1970s.[2] In the two acts of *The Secretary Bird* (1967), novelist Hugh Walford discovers that his wife has been unfaithful and is about to elope with a stockbroker called John Brownlow. Generously, the husband offers to take the blame for the divorce (an act of *in flagrante* infidelity was needed according to the British code of law of the time) and invites his wife's lover, as well as his own attractive secretary, to spend a day and a night at the Walfords' home – so that he can meet his wife's new partner and commit the necessary adultery with his subordinate. Before the end, however, it becomes apparent that all along his plan has been to make his wife jealous, as well as to undermine her relationship with Brownlow. He succeeds, and in the end the Walfords are seen playing cards exactly as in the opening scene, all outsiders gone.

Even a short recapitulation of the source and target plots reveals that in order to make the play presentable on stage, the Italian producers have had to make a number of geographical and cultural changes. In Barbareschi's *L'anatra all'arancia*, the British novelist of *The Secretary Bird* becomes a TV presenter from northern Italy, and his rival is no longer a dynamic city stockbroker, but a fascinating Russian man with aristocratic blood and large estates. These in themselves are telltale signs that, notwithstanding its presence on the bill, Douglas Home's title is not being treated as important cultural capital: it is hard to imagine the plot of a Pinter or Stoppard play being similarly relocated and tweaked, particularly if a direct interlingual dependence has been publicly announced.

When the attention is shifted from the setting to the finer facts of invention and disposition, however, it becomes apparent that the Italian changes are much more frequent and pervasive. To list a few examples from a far ampler repertory: the Walfords have a governess, Mrs Gray, while the Ferraris have a sort of butler, Ernesto Russo; at the very beginning of the play, the British couple are playing a card game (Douglas Home 1969: 1), while their Italian counterparts have just concluded a game of chess; in Act One, Scene 2 of *The Secretary Bird*, the two male rivals are said to have just played a game of golf together (Douglas Home 1969: 20), whereas in *L'anatra all'arancia* they discuss a game of tennis; again in Act One, Scene 2, Ms Forsyth gets 'bogged down on the croquet lawn in her high heels' (Douglas Home 1969: 24), while in the Italian version the secretary, Chanel Pizziconi, gets bitten by a wasp in the garden; at the beginning of Act Two, the two couples are seen playing bridge in Douglas Home's play (1969: 33) and charades in the Italian stage production; at the end of the play, Liz Walford is crying (Douglas Home 1969: 64), whereas Lisa Ferrari is laughing.[3]

The distance between the two texts is just as considerable if viewed through the lens of close reading. As said above, in the opening scene of *The Secretary Bird*, the Walfords are playing a game of cards, at the end of which the husband obtains from his wife an implicit admission of betrayal. Hugh asks Liz whether she had lunch at the hairdresser's, and she replies that she did:

> HUGH. Never ring your wife up at the hairdresser a fellow once told me –
>   because she won't be there.
> LIZ. Did you ring me?
> HUGH. No. […] What's his name?
> LIZ […] John Brownlow. (Douglas Home 1969: 1–2)

The whole initial exchange is very concise, and never strays from the commonplace (counting the points after a game of cards, having a drink) until the husband offers a second-hand remark about the wisdom of ringing one's wife at the hairdresser. When Liz reacts by asking whether he did ring her at the hairdresser, he just utters a monosyllabic negative – leaving her and us in doubt as to whether he was just bluffing or is now breaching the maxim of quality (i.e. lying openly to create an implicature; Grice 1991: 22–57). Either way, the presupposition or the implicature is that Liz has been unfaithful. Making another appeal to her inferencing abilities, Hugh asks her to give him a name, and she complies. With a minimum of fuss and comment, the premise of the whole play has been established.

A comparison of that scene with its Italian counterpart leaves one wondering about the exact association of Barbareschi's mise-en-scène with Douglas Home's text:

> LISA: Hey – they are the best beauticians in Milan. It was a good thing I had
>   made an appointment, too, because it was so, so crowded.
> GILBERTO: Ah? Firefighters, I guess?

LISA: Firefighters? Why?

GILBERTO: There was a fire!

LISA: A fire?

GILBERTO: Yes – they said so on TV. All the building above the beauticians went up in flames. I thought you'd noticed – unless you thought the smell of burning was because of the hair and the wax.

LISA: Any victims?

GILBERTO: Just one – here he is. (*Hands her the drink*)

LISA: Oh God, I'm sorry. Look, I'm really sorry, Gilberto. I should have told you everything a long time ago.

GILBERTO: Don't worry. Television is where I work. It's only right that I should learn I'm a cuckold from a TV set. Who's the winner?

LISA: Volodia. Volodia Smirnov.[4]

The differences are numerous. In the English version, as seen above, this particular exchange is very short (twenty-eight words in all, four turns at talk) and resolved by means of presupposition and implicature, rather than explicit admission. The Italian version is almost four times longer (108 words distributed along 10 turns) and generally more explicit – though Lisa has to understand at least one implicature, when her husband breaches the maxim of quality by referring to himself as the only victim of the fire. While Liz Walford responds to her husband's direct question by providing a name, Lisa Ferrari prefaces the admission by apologizing rather profusely, and saying that she should have told him everything a long time before. Analogously, Gilberto Ferrari is much more explicit and loquacious than his English counterpart: he calls himself 'a cuckold', and asks who 'the winner' is. Finally, in *L'anatra all'arancia*, even the facts are more eloquent than in *The Secretary Bird*: the beauticians who replace the original hairdressers are almost burnt to the ground in order to make Lisa Ferrari's cover story untenable.

One could, of course, attribute the bulk of these differences to the different conditions of 1960s Britain and contemporary Italian culture. Various studies have demonstrated that even in textual translations, Italians tend to make explicit what is implicit in English writing (Venturi 2011: 217–72), and that Italian translations of British humour have a marked tendency towards clarity, explanation and gap-filling (Morini 2013b: 135–46). Here, in other words, the Italian translators might simply be trying to make the play more palatable for Italian audiences in the 2010s. However, if that explanation seems valid for certain details in the Italian production – the references to contemporary sports and politics with which the text is peppered throughout, for instance – it sounds less than satisfactory for some of the most marked modifications of dialogue and situation. Why, for instance, if the opening card game has been deemed to be unfashionable, does the Italian couple play chess? And if the rest of the show is similarly reviewed: why do the Italian characters play charades with classical references? Why is the governess of the source turned into a butler in the translation?

The answers to these questions become simple enough when one stops looking at the simple pair formed by target play/performance and pretended source text, and investigates what turns out to be a rather complicated history of intertextual, intralingual and intersemiotic transmission. The main clue to uncovering that story lies in the Italian title: it is in fact very hard to say – in interlingual terms alone – why *The Secretary Bird* turns into *L'anatra all'arancia*. It is true that a duck à l'orange is said to be in preparation at the end of Act One of the Italian performance; but no such dish is mentioned in the English play, and there is no literal or metaphorical relationship of the dish or its name with the titular English bird.[5] The reason for this is that *L'anatra all'arancia* is not really a new title in Italian culture. In fact, if one uses a search engine to look up that string of text, the first results obtained refer not to the theatrical production under discussion here, but to an Italian movie released in 1975, directed by Luciano Salce and starring Ugo Tognazzi and Monica Vitti. The fact that this was quite a popular film at the time is surely enough to explain why Barbareschi's company decided to stick with its title.

Does this mean that the production of the 2010s is really a translation of the Italian movie, rather than of the English play? The answer is mostly negative. Though markedly different from Douglas Home's *The Secretary Bird*, Salce's film does not offer anything more than a superficial resemblance to Barbareschi's production. In general, the 1975 *Anatra all'arancia* looks like a sexed-up, more comic version of the same story. In 1970s Italian cinema, sex comedies showing naked body parts of attractive young actresses were much in vogue – and in this case, it is Barbara Bouchet in the role of the young, uninhibited secretary who is tasked with providing that form of entertainment. Admittedly, there are some convergences between the plot of the film and that of the Italian production – the wasp incident, and obviously the titular duck à l'orange – but these are developed in a very different fashion, and a lot of events and exchanges in the movie find no parallel either in the English play or on the Italian stage.

The reason for these intriguing similarities and marked differences is that the script of Salce's film is not the intralingual source text for Barbareschi's production – but both depend on a common source that is neither Italian nor English. During the opening credits, the script of the movie is attributed to Bernardino Zapponi, who is said to have adapted the 'comedy of the same title by William Douglas Home and Marc Gilbert Sauvajon' ('Tratto dall'omonima commedia di William Douglas Home / Marc Gilbert Sauvajon'). Sauvajon was a French playwright, many of whose theatrical successes were translations of English plays – like *Le Canard à l'orange*, written some time before 1974 and famously televised in France in 1979. Somehow, this version immediately crossed the Alps, because a handful of Italian libraries still bear traces of a production of 'L'anitra all'arancia: Two Acts by W. Douglas and M. Gilbert Sauvajon' (Douglas Home, Sauvajon, and Marino 1974) presented for the theatrical season 1974/5. This Italian script was 'adapted' ('riduzione italiana di') by Nino Marino, the production directed by Alberto Lionello.[6] It is apparently impossible to find written or audiovisual testimonies of this version, but the exact correspondence of the titles and the presence of the name of the French translator, as well as the fortunes that followed for the play in Italy, indicate rather unambiguously that this was a translation from the French intermediate text, rather than from its English prime source. After all, French was the most widely known foreign language in Italy at the time, and an Italian theatre company would have had fewer difficulties working on Sauvajon's script.

That *The Secretary Bird* reached Italy by way of France, and never really recovered anything approaching its original English form, can be easily proved by comparing the plot and dialogue of *Le Canard à l'orange* with that of the various versions of *L'anatra all'arancia*. Fortunately, while Douglas Home's play has become a historical footnote of British theatre history, the French version has been successful enough to grant a recent re-publication, and can also be watched online in various productions, including the 1979 mise-en-scène for television.[7] A quick scan reveals that all the Italian scenes which stray from the English textual source (the charades, the wasp incident, the laughing ending) are based on the French play. The smallest micro-linguistic sample suffices to confirm that the Italian dialogue, whatever its further intralingual adjustments, is ultimately dependent on interlingual translation from the French:

LIZ: The fire?
HUGH: I thought you'd noticed. They said on the radio that the whole building had to be evacuated. [...] Don't worry, apparently I'm the only victim.
LIZ: I'm so sorry, Hugh ... I should have told you everything a long time ago, but ...
HUGH: I work at the BBC, dear ... It's only normal that it should be the radio who tells me I'm a cuckold ... What's the winner's name?
LIZ: Hugh Brownlow.[8]

Though there are some missing links in the chain of textual transmission, it is now possible to hazard an approximate reconstruction of the process leading from the English play to its latest Italian theatre translation. In 1967, *The Secretary Bird* was presented on the English stage, and a printed version of the play was published in 1969. Sometime between 1969 and 1974, Marc-Gilbert Sauvajon, a playwright who 'approaches the English texts he habitually works on in the manner of an author rather than of a translator',[9] produced a French version. In 1974, a first Italian theatre translation appeared on stage that was clearly dependent on Sauvajon (*L'anitra all'arancia*). It is impossible to establish whether the first Italian production kept the English setting (with which Sauvajon, in spite of all his modifications of plot and dialogue, had decided to keep faith); what is certain is that the 1975 Italian film, which was still partly based on the French intermediate text, is set in Italy – as are all the subsequent Italian versions about which it is possible to unearth any kind of information. Thus, when Barbareschi and his company decided to prepare a new production of *L'anatra all'arancia* around 2016, they used as a textual source either the French original or, more probably, a script which had been circulating for decades in Italian theatrical circles, still ultimately based on Sauvajon's work. This appears to be confirmed by the fact that in Barbareschi's production, the male protagonist's name is Gilberto Ferrari – and whereas Ugo Tognazzi's character in the movie is called Livio Stefani, there are scripts and productions retrievable online which predate Barbareschi's, and where the husband bears the same name as in the 2016 version.[10]

In short, Barbareschi's company probably worked on an old Italian script, adding some modernizing details (Holmes 1988: 37) and giving a Russian identity to the glamorous lover. Whether they also compared that script with the French and English plays is almost impossible to say – in the one case because the whole Italian tradition is dependent on Sauvajon's version, in the other because there are no evident traces of Douglas Home's prime source in the 2016 production. Also, although this is impossible to prove, it seems quite likely that the company had the 1975 film in mind, if only in intersemiotic terms: the fact that they decided to turn Douglas Home's and Sauvajon's governess (Mrs/Mme Grey) into a butler from southern Italy (Ernesto Russo) might owe something to the film, which featured a male Neapolitan servant. Certainly, the 1975 film is the main reason why the title of this production is *L'anatra all'arancia*: choosing something closer to the English pun might have alienated the older audiences who had watched the film on the big screen, and calling it by the original Italian name of *L'anitra all'arancia* might have given the impression of a literary, somewhat old-fashioned play.

Naturally, all these processes are quite common in the domain of theatre translation. What is significant, in this rather complex scenario of indirect translation and intersemiotic influences, is that Barbareschi's company decided to declare, at one stage of their promotional campaign, that their prime source was the 'text' of the English play. Since very few Italian theatregoers might have been expected to know anything about Douglas Home's *The Secretary Bird*, that declaration can only point to the ideological power of the single source, and generally of text-centric translation norms – not enough to lead the theatre company to actually translate the English play, but enough to make them say that they had done so.

7.3 *Covert intra-/intersemiotic translation:* The War of the Roses/La Guerra dei Roses

In November 2016, an Italian theatre company directed by Filippo Dini, and starring well-known TV personality Ambra Angiolini as the female protagonist, started touring an Italian version of *The War of the Roses* – not a dramatic account of fifteenth-century dynastic turmoil and civil strife, but a story in which a married couple (the titular Roses) stop loving each other, start bickering over their worldly possessions and end up fighting each other to death. The playbill for this production is relatively simple: against a background of flowery wallpaper standing for the domestic setting of the play, the female and male protagonists, dressed in white T-shirts, fix a serious gaze upon the viewer. Apart from the names of these two actors, printed in white reverse type on a blood-red stain above the title, the only other strings of words which are clearly legible from a distance are the title itself – the most foregrounded piece of writing in the whole image – and the names of Filippo Dini and Warren Adler. Adler, as evidenced by type size and position (just below the title), is the author.

Once that fact is univocally established, however, the problem of identifying a source begins – because *The War of the Roses* has a rather complex history of intersemiotic as well as interlingual versions. A novel bearing that title was published at the beginning of the 1980s (Adler 1981). At the end of the decade, the novel was turned into a film starring Kathleen Turner and Michael Douglas, with a script written by Michael J. Leeson (DeVito 1989). This film was so successful, and remained so firmly planted in the collective imagination, that close to three decades later, Warren Adler turned the story into a play (Adler 2008).

In a promotional press conference held at the Teatro Manzoni in Milan on 11 November 2016[11] and now retrievable online, three of the actors involved appeared to take it for granted that the prime source for their production was its original, novelistic version. In her initial presentation of *La guerra dei Roses* and her motives for taking part, Ambra Angiolini admitted that she was worried because 'it was a film, it was a novel, it was all too much' ('Era un film, era un romanzo, era tutto troppo': 1.30 mins); a few minutes later, she asked the audience whether any of them had read the novel ('Qualcuno di voi ha letto il romanzo?': 6.15 mins). During the whole conference, there were various mentions of Adler's name, as well as some references to the novel and the film. Adler's play, by contrast, was never mentioned.[12] This appeared to imply that the 2016 *La guerra dei Roses* was an independent theatre translation of the 1981 novel – perhaps with intersemiotic nods to the 1989 film – rather than a production based on an interlingual version of the 2008 play.

However, a bare glance at that play is enough to show that it was the main inspiration for the Italian theatre translation. This can be illustrated by looking at the scenes in which the protagonists first appear across all the literary, cinematic and theatrical versions. In the novel, the first chapter tells the story of how Barbara and Jonathan, still at university, meet at an auction on Cape Cod and bicker over a Staffordshire figurine of a pugilist. In the film, the meeting between the two is shown after an opening scene in which Danny DeVito, playing the part of a divorce lawyer and acting as narrator, presents the whole as a sort of moral exemplum (the dialogue in the auction scene is a bit different, and the pugilist becomes a Shinto goddess). In the English play and the Italian production, however, before their first meeting is enacted, the two protagonists are presented on a dimly lit stage – this, the tone they adopt and what they say all gives the impression that they are already dead and trying to present their cases retrospectively in front of a higher authority.

> JONATHAN [...] I'm not saying I'm blameless. But as God is my witness. Sorry about that. I meant no disrespect. [...]
> BARBARA [...] As a general rule, men are stupid. Okay, they were created first. It was your choice [...]
>
> (Adler 2008: Act 1 Scene 1, 1–2)[13]

As a rule, any Italian spectator who had already had the opportunity to read the English play could have recognized a great number of scenes which – give or take the odd intralingual or intrasemiotic modification – reproduced Adler's 2008 dramatic version very closely. But if at this stage it seems strange that the Italian company did not choose to declare the dependence of their production on Adler's play, it has to be pointed out that this degree of closeness was not maintained throughout. The exchange quoted above, for instance, comes at the very beginning of William Adler's 2008 play; in the Italian production, by contrast, it was only acted out after a sort of prologue in which the two divorce lawyers of the couple (Goldstein and Thurmont) had already introduced the situation in philosophical, quasi-metaphysical terms – one of them pointing at the possibility of (eternal?) salvation for the bickering couple. The inclusion of this scene might reflect the Italians' willingness to open a very dark play on a more hopeful note. More generally, however, it shows that – as is perfectly understandable in theatre translation – the generic attribution of authorship to 'William Adler' does not exclude the possibility of interpolation.

This was evident in other loci and features of the target production, where the Italians did not necessarily add whole exchanges, but modified characters and scenes in a subtler way. Most often, it appears that it was their intention to make contrasts clearer and sharper. This motivation is apparent enough in the Italian stage version of the auction scene detailed above – the one that opens the novel and is presented in all versions as a key to understanding the protagonists and their relationship. In the novel, the film and the English play, the development of the auction undergoes various modifications, but it is always the case that Barbara outbids her future husband – which means that their relationship is shown to be built on competitiveness and strife from the very beginning. The people responsible for the Italian production, by contrast, decided to create a sharper, more Manichaean contrast between initial harmony and final disintegration. In *La guerra dei Roses*, therefore, it is made clear from the very beginning that Barbara is buying the second, matching figurine for Jonathan, having decided to outbid another customer because she understands that completing the pair is important to him.

Apart from these and other Italian contributions, there are some aspects and scenes in the theatre translation which denounce, more or less openly, the influence of the DeVito movie. Structurally, the idea of showing the divorce lawyers as a sort of chorus, commenting and philosophizing on what is going on with the bickering couple, may owe something to the role of lawyer/narrator played by DeVito himself in the film. But while for general questions such as this it is difficult to determine the debt owed by one version to another, in the case of dialogue, establishing filiation may be much easier. One scene of *La guerra dei Roses*, in particular, has no direct equivalent or obvious blueprint in any of the versions directly authored by Adler, and is clearly a calque of the film. Towards the end of their matrimonial war, and just before the final battle which will put paid to their marriage and their lives, Jonathan and Barbara, still living together in a partitioned house, meet on a staircase and exchange volleys of insults:

OLIVER Stupid bitch.
BARBARA You bastard.
OLIVER Slut.
BARBARA Scum.
OLIVER Filth.
BARBARA Faggot. (DeVito 1989: 74.05 mins)

This passage perfectly illustrates the free use of interlingual and intersemiotic sources in the Italian theatre translation. The rapid exchange of English insults is closely reproduced in Italian, with the exact same timing and very similar derogatory terms. The situation in which the exchange takes place is also a close intersemiotic version of the film – the two characters meet on a staircase in both DeVito (1989) and the 2016 *La guerra dei Roses*. Both in the film and in the Italian production, at the end of the exchange the couple meet a servant whom they greet courteously – which creates a comic contrast with their behaviour to each other. However, while the origin of this scene is clear, the Italian producers have fitted it into a different *fabula* and a different set of characters: as shown in the transcription, the name of the male protagonist in the film is Oliver, while the Italian producers keep 'Jonathan' from the novel and the play;[14] the female servant the two meet in the film (Susan) is turned into a man in the Italian stage version (Donald); and the Italian scenes which are staged before and after this one are completely different from those in the movie.

In sum, the 2016 Italian theatre translation of *The War of the Roses* is almost as complex as a target theatre act as it is in terms of the history of its sources. If most of the dialogue is an interlingual translation of the 2008 play, some changes hail from the 1989 film and some are probably intralingual interpolations. The same can be said in terms of stage presentation and scene disposition: the 2008 play is the main intrasemiotic source, but some intersemiotic interferences from the film are traceable and some characters and situations have been added or modified by the Italian company. Ultimately, it is perfectly justifiable to present the Italian performances as stemming from 'William Adler', as the playbill does: no single English version can be identified as a unique inspiration.

Given this complex filiation history, the actors' behaviour in the press conference may appear inexplicable: why do they fail to mention the stage play, and why do they repeatedly and favourably refer to the novel – i.e. to the only version of the story that appears to have had no direct influence on their production? The answer is probably twofold, having to do with both the enduring cultural prestige of printed literature in this visual age and the cogency of the single-source norm. Instinctively, the actors may feel that it is important to identify, if not a single source, at least a source that is more important than the others. The novel has the double advantage of being 'the original' (the first version of the story) and belonging to a more durable, prestigious fictional form than that of theatrical performance. Therefore, whether they know or not that most of their dialogue is derived from the 2008 play, and that some scenes have been added and some have been taken from the 1989 film, they think it best to present the earliest version of *The War of the Roses* as their prime inspiration.

7.4 Conclusion: Performative realities and text-centric ideologies

As anticipated in the first section of this chapter, the various approximations, adjustments and detours that lead from Douglas Home's *Secretary Bird* to a recent Italian production of *L'anatra all'arancia*, and from the theatrical version of William Adler's *The War of the Roses* to its Italian production, are quite common in theatre translation. A company's first consideration is for the effectiveness of the play and the favourable reaction of the audience: once these two boxes are ticked, a low level of priority is assigned to keeping faith with a source (with any source). However, while the various intermediate dependencies of *L'anatra all'arancia* and *La guerra dei Roses* are interesting in themselves, it is more interesting to note that they are either glossed over or denied. As noted in the first section, theatre translation appears to combine great freedom of selection with a number of text-centric ideological constraints.

If the analyses of the above section are seen as answers to one of Toury's questions ('is indirect translation permitted at all?'), the answer appears to be that in the world of theatre, indirect translation is practised but not permitted – or permitted but viewed unfavourably. In this, theatre translation behaves much in the same manner as translation from little-known or exotic languages – though the underlying reasons are slightly different. The publishers who print indirect translations of Russian or Chinese texts, for instance, do so because there is a scarcity of translators from those languages (Bauer 1999; Ghini 2017). The translators/producers/directors/actors who modify previous existing translations of a play, or interpolate scenes from previous intra- or intersemiotic versions, probably do so to speed up the process and to produce a recognizable, attractive target theatre act.

This similarity, and the widespread use of indirect derivation in the world of theatre, leads one back to the text/performance dichotomy that has dominated theatrical translation discourse up to a couple of decades ago. If the process is observed from the viewpoint of performance, it is quite normal for theatre translation to be spurious and indirect. On the other hand, as seen in Chapter 6, the late-Renaissance inclusion of drama in the domain of literature has led to an infusion of prestige – and that prestige also implies a number of obligations. Contemporary theatre producers, directors and actors know perfectly well that their popularity and livelihood depend on the appreciation of their final performance, not on the exact replication of a single source. But they also know intuitively that a demonstrable dependence on a single textual source will still be perceived as a positive value by most theatregoers – that their freedom as theatre translators, in other words, can only be maintained if it is hidden in plain sight.

Performance as translation, translation in performance: Two examples from contemporary experimental theatre

Independently of their complex stage and intertextual histories, all the theatre translations considered in Chapter 7 are based, at least partly, on traditional plays aimed at directing dialogue and mise-en-scène. The corresponding analyses, therefore, have a strong inter- and intralingual emphasis, even though the other levels of theatre translation are always considered. This chapter looks at two contemporary works in which text, for different reasons, does not occupy the same central position – and in which, consequently, the effects of inter- and intrasemiotic translation are much more prominent. In §8.2, two productions of Heiner Müller's *Hamletmaschine* are described which make it clear that even though interlingual translation still plays a small part (one of the companies is American, the other is French, while the source text is German), the two target theatre acts are steered in different directions by different intersemiotic choices. In §8.3, *Birdie*, a recent multimedia production by the Catalan company Agrupación Señor Serrano, is presented as an example of how theatrical spectacle is not only – inevitably – the product of translation, but can also incorporate and foreground translation processes within the very fabric of its performance.

8.1 Theatre translation, theatre as translation

It has been said in Part II that the production of any target theatre act may involve all or some of the four aspects of theatre translation – but so far the first, interlingual level of description has been present, and sometimes dominant, in the case studies. However, if all the consequences of the model outlined in Part II are accepted, it must be pointed out that the presence of interlingual transformation is not necessary for a theatre act to be a theatre translation. In other words – as an age-old commonplace and all 'text to stage' book series testify (see, for instance, Kennan and Tempera 1992; and from a theoretical standpoint, Laera 2019: 18–25) – theatrical performance is itself a form of translation. Shakespeare writes *Much Ado About Nothing* having in mind the actors of his company and some kind of stage realization (so much so that after a while he starts using the name of an actor, 'Kemp', instead of that of a character, 'Dogberry'). Though he may know the style of his associates perfectly well, the actors will then impose their interpretation on the text from the very first rehearsal, and in a successful run of performances, lines will be changed, added or dropped depending on audiences' reactions. Even in the very unlikely event that no syllable of the initial script is actually changed, the arrangement or use of props, a shrill tone or an ironic inflection will create different interpretive possibilities. And when the original company is no longer in existence, when *Much Ado About Nothing* is remade by English-speaking companies in the following centuries, every new performance will inevitably involve new intralingual and inter- and intrasemiotic adjustments. Every new performance, in theory, will be amenable to analysis as a target theatre act.

The fact that every performance is a new theatre translation becomes more evident when non-traditional theatrical productions are considered. The very different works analysed in Chapters 7 and 8 have at least this in common – that however spectacular (*Il pastor fido*) or technological (*La guerra dei Roses*) their actual realizations may be, they all revolve around a written text that dictates much of what gets said and a lot of what happens on stage. But if many theatrical seasons of the Western World are still filled with this kind of fare, it is important to remember that other, less text-centric kinds of spectacle have always been around, and some of them have acquired the status of cultural capital in the last century. In the second half of the twentieth century, after early experimentation within the European avant-garde (Bay-Cheng 2007) and the revolutions brought about by Artaud and Brecht, among others, various forms of theatre arose in which the written word had a much less central or normative position than in the previous half millennium.[1] One need only think of the big 'intercultural' productions, or of the various manifestations of what has been variously called 'postmodern', 'experimental' or – with a tautology much in vogue today – 'contemporary' theatre. All these labels reflect different periods, genres and types of production, the precise definition of which lies beyond the scope of this monograph; what is interesting for present purposes is observing what happens when one of these works gets performed far from its place of origin.

Paradoxically enough, one work that started out as mere text is perfect for this kind of observation. Heiner Müller's *Hamletmaschine* is a very short and occult script that inevitably requires a lot of interpretation at the level of intersemiotic translation: every new mise-en-scène, therefore, can easily be seen as entirely different product. And even when the text has to be turned into another language, as happens in the American and French productions analysed below, it is immediately apparent that the interlingual passage is the least important part of the whole process of theatre translation.

The fact that theatrical spectacle is not only a form of translation, but can also involve translation in its very fabric, is evident in certain recent shows which involve the audience in their realization, employ a variety of live and recorded media and present the same concepts in different modes. Some of these shows incorporate the contributions of those that Schechner (2013: 250) calls 'partakers', translate them on stage in visible/audible form and mix them up with the work of 'sourcers', 'producers' and 'performers' (see Cerratto-Pargman, Rossitto and Barkhuus 2014). Others, like the multimedia performance analysed here, are less open in terms of audience participation, but show the workings of on-stage translation (at all levels) in exemplary fashion.

8.2 *Performance as translation: Heiner Müller's* Hamletmaschine

When he wrote the text of *Die Hamletmaschine* (first published in 1977), Heiner Müller had been translating and transforming Shakespeare for a while – including a German version of *Hamlet* – for the theatrical audiences of the German Democratic Republic. Thus, broadly speaking, this short modernist script was a translation, arising out of his own closer interlingual transformation of the Shakespearean play and exploiting Shakespearean themes and characters in order to create what seems to amount to a meditation on socialism, modern politics, the split self and the mechanization of society. It is rather paradoxical that this work – which went on to become one of the most popular in the canon of experimental, performance-driven theatre – can be seen as exquisitely textual in its first inception. The reasons for this are both practical and intrinsic. On the one hand, *Die Hamletmaschine* was published (in West Germany, and in a programme for another play by Müller; Barnett 2016: 5) some years before it was performed. On the other hand, if taken literally, it was unworkable as a theatrical script, and sounded more like a prose poem in T. S. Eliot's *Waste Land* tradition than anything out of Beckett's dramatic repertoire (Barnett 2014):

> Ich war Hamlet. Ich stand an der Küste und redete mit der Brandung BLABLA, im Rücken die Ruinen von Europa.
>
> (Girshausen 1978: 11)

> I was Hamlet. I stood on the coast and spoke with the surf BLABLA, the ruins of Europe behind me.

As illustrated by this short quotation, *Die Hamletmaschine* is essentially dramatic monologue – though, as reflected in the variety of choices adopted by different productions, and because of the multiplicity of real and made-up quotations with which it is interspersed (Barnett 2016: 28), it is not always clear who is speaking the lines. Insofar as it can be considered as a theatrical monologue (spoken by one or more voices, as will be seen below), it is a relatively short one, at around 2,000 words. While there is no doubting that the text is somehow presented as a play, however – it is divided into five 'Acts', and its register is colloquial[2] – its indefiniteness of voice is not the only reason why Müller's work is confusing and open-ended in theatrical terms. Another source of performative difficulty resides in the stage directions, which are often impossible to follow if taken literally and therefore invite some kind of metaphorical interpretation or technological solution ('Tiefsee. Ophelia im Rollstuhl. Frische Trümmer Leichen und Leichenteile treiben vorbei'; 'Deep sea. Ophelia in a wheelchair. Fresh rubble, corpses and pieces of corpses pass by'; Girshausen 1978: 23). In short, *Die Hamletmaschine* can only be seen as guiding theatrical performance in the same sense as Morton Feldman's or John Cage's graphic notation can be considered as a guide for singers and musicians (Boutwell 2012).

This open-endedness has led theatre producers to devise a wide variety of intersemiotic solutions in terms of mise-en-scène, speaking roles and interpretation of the stage directions. Some features, either because they were easier to stage or because they were strongly suggested by the text, have been common to all or most productions. A great number of companies, for instance, have decided to set the words of the play against a backdrop of postmodern, mechanistic urban squalor and/or to suggest the idea of mechanical alienation by means of movement and choreography. Also, many directors have tended to realize in a simple, unmediated manner those few stage directions which look less problematic and ambiguous on paper – most notably, the one in the fourth act asking the 'Hamletperformer' to tear up a photograph of the writer (Girshausen 1978: 21). Finally, and most obviously, the element that has been common to all performances is *Die Hamletmaschine* itself – the text, whether in German or in translation, told by one person or a multiplicity of actors, spoken directly by humans and/or presented as a disembodied recording.

One of the earliest stage versions of the play was also one of the most celebrated: Robert Wilson's English-language *Hamletmachine* was, in fact, so successful that it acquired a life of its own, was widely studied in the academic world and was recently reprised in Europe by the American director himself. Here, however, the first production is summarized with the help of contemporary reviews (Rogoff 1986), near-contemporary appraisals (Zurbrugg 1988) and a recent scholarly description (Barnett 2016: 50–5).

Wilson used as actors a group of fourteen or fifteen students[3] from New York University, who were instructed to perform a certain number of repeated, mechanized movements. This complicated sequence, involving only a few props such as chairs and a table (Rogoff 1986: 55), lasted twenty minutes and was first presented in dumb show (Barnett 2016: 50). After its first realization, all the actors rotated by 90 degrees, and the sequence was repeated – this time during a rendition of the words of the first 'Act' ('Family album' – 'Familienalbum'). The same sequence, with another rotation, was again performed for the second part of the play ('Europe of the woman' – 'Das Europa der Frau'). The third part ('Scherzo') had the actors looking from the stage at a pre-recorded film of their mechanized movements on screen. The rotations began afresh with the two concluding 'Acts' ('Pest in Buda/Battle of Greenland' – 'Pest in Buda/Schlacht um Grönland'; and 'Maddening Endurance/Inside the Dreaded Armour/Millennia' – 'Wildharrend/In der furchtbaren Rüstung/ Jahrtausende'). By means of this rigidly choreographed organization, Wilson created the impression of modern machinery without any need for machines, and at the same time conferred a circularity to the whole – because at the end of the show, after four rotations, the actors would be realigned with their initial positions. The realization of the central 'Act' as a film within the play could thus be said to have three different functions or consequences: firstly, it evoked the play-within-the-play episode in *Hamlet*; secondly, it identified 'Scherzo' as the still heart at the centre of an ever-rotating, assembly-line kind of world; thirdly, it was mathematically necessary if a single full rotation had to be realized.

In this rather long automated version, it is interesting to see what happened to Heiner Müller's words. Since the sequence of movements was always the same, only taking place along different axes, the spoken word had to be accommodated within the performers' movements. The five acts of *Hamletmaschine* being of different lengths, certain sections had to be stretched, while others had to be told quickly, almost in truncated form (Barnett 2016: 51). Therefore, while the interlingual translation was a close one and no parts were cut or added, its intersemiotic stage realization was heavily interventionist. Language was made to be subservient to performance, in this and in other ways – for instance, by allowing the actors to speak only after the first dumb-show completion of their mechanized routine. Though by these means linguistic utterances were made to feel as automated as the performers' movements, there were also occasions on which they arguably took precedence over other forms of expression. In 'Pest in Buda', for instance, the stage directions were spoken by the female performers and were 'thus allowed to unfold in the audience's imagination and not on stage' (again, all of them except the one calling for Heiner Müller's photograph to be torn up; Barnett 2016: 53).

Another intersemiotic way in which dramatic language lost weight – at least the traditional weight of personal expression – was by dint of a refusal to identify a single monologist or a limited number of soliloquizing actors. In Wilson's *Hamletmachine*, the lines were sometimes delivered by a single actor, sometimes distributed among different performers, sometimes screeched, sometimes uttered in neutral tones. On occasion, several actors sitting at a table would speak their lines in non-matching voices. In short, no attempt was made to explain Müller's text, or to make it less strange, either by theatrical illustration or through the unifying value of human acting. As most contemporary observers and later commentators pointed out, and as Heiner Müller himself noted approvingly, 'Wilson's productions remain radically open' (Barnett 2016: 54) and leave the audience 'free to make [their] own associations' (Zurbrugg 1988: 56).

Of course, the openness created by means of intersemiotic translation is not the same kind of openness that obtains when *Die Hamletmaschine* is simply read. On the one hand, new kinds of tantalizing, freely interpretable strangeness are created; on the other, the weirdness of the text will at times be normalized or interpreted by the performers. A straightforward example of this has to do with the fact that in the source play, the German prose is occasionally interrupted by lines of English verse in block letters, approximating iambic pentameters and sounding like quotations (but being mostly a jumble of Shakespearean, biblical and heterogeneous allusions):

AH THE WHOLE GLOBE FOR A REAL SORROW
RICHARD THE THIRD I THE PRINCEKILLING KING

(Girshausen 1978: 11)

The fact that Wilson's is an English-speaking performance imposes the loss of this kind of *Verfremdung* – though analogous forms of estrangement can be produced by the acoustic, visual or kinetic modes when the lines are uttered.

Translations of the text in languages other than English, of course, do not create this particular form of interlingual normalization. This is the case of a recent French theatre translation of *Die Hamletmaschine*, co-produced by Scènes Théâtre Cinéma and Neither Nor, directed by David Mambouch and Philippe Vincent and presented in Lyon at the beginning of 2016. In this case, when the first English lines are heard, the impression of estrangement is retained, even heightened by the strong French accent in which they are delivered. Here as in Wilson's translation, however, the audience feel that language has lost its primacy in the world of theatre. The opening words of Müller's text are spoken forty minutes into the show:

J'étais Hamlet. Je me trouvais sur le rivage et je parlais avec le ressac [Pause] Blah, blah. [Pause: seagulls screeching]. BLAH, BLAH [Pause: seagulls screeching]. BLAH [Pause]. Les cloches annonçaient les funérailles nationales.

I was Hamlet. I stood on the coast and spoke with the surf. Blah, Blah. BLAH, BLAH. BLAH. The bells were announcing the state funerals.[4]

As for the text itself, a number of small intralingual additions and modifications – as well as intersemiotic tweaks – are observable which are a healthy reminder of the volatile nature of theatre translation. First of all, the Eliot-like passage 'im Rücken die Ruinen von Europa' (The ruins of Europe behind me) is expunged – though in the absence of other documentation about this production, it is impossible to say whether that was just a memory lapse or a conscious choice.[5] Secondly, the pauses and repetitions in the monologue, as well as the tone and demeanour of the male actor (Philippe Vincent, the 'Hamletperformer' and one of the two directors) uttering those few words, amount to an interpretation of Müller's very open text. 'Blah, Blah' gets repeated and, given that the actor's voice is raised after the first repetition and his head turns when he hears the sound of seagulls, one assumes that the successive repetitions become responses to the birds' screeching. Finally, and inevitably, even the general attitude of the actor (serious, almost ominous), his costume and the objects he is carrying (he is in furs, with a top hat on his head and a guitar in his hand), as well as the general appearance of the stage (see next paragraph) and the soundtrack (wind, surf, seagulls), contribute to creating an impression in the viewer and shape the significance of the monologue the Hamletperformer is delivering.

The multimodal, performative, non-verbal part of this translation takes precedence over the spoken rendition of the text. In the forty minutes preceding these words, the audience are first presented with an empty stage lit by a single spotlight and run through by sheets of paper, shopping bags and other kinds of debris that are blown about by an artificial wind. After a few minutes of this, five actors begin roaming the stage, pushing and pulling cumbersome objects, shouting and making gestures. Among other performative events, one male actor is dug up and out of a trap by a female actor, like Lazarus being dragged out of the grave; another bald-headed female actor is seen and heard strutting around on stage and laughing maniacally; various kinds of armed and unarmed confrontations between actors take place. This is a very shortened summary, as it would take too much space to describe all the micro-events before the beginning of scripted talk. However, it may be relevant to point out that after about twenty minutes, the actors start to collaborate in an improvised assembly line (one of them is dressed like a construction worker, with an orange jacket on and a safety helmet on her head), and end up erecting a rather complicated structure which looks as if it is made up of all the debris of twentieth-century urban civilization (wooden planks, wooden containers, various metal objects, chairs). Again, the 'machine' side of *Hamletmaschine* is realized intersemiotically, by means of stagecraft, before a single word of Müller's text is spoken. While in Wilson's production it is the alienation of repetitive human movements that creates the impression of a mechanized world, here it is the enormous quantity of objects stacked up on stage which forms an image of dilapidated modernity (Keim 1998: 63–9). While both translations attempt to tease out some of the implications in the text, it is evident that their intersemiotic strategies are very different, and that these different strategies create very different impressions when the text is spoken by the actors. In Wilson's *Hamletmachine*, the words sound as if they are uttered by puppets or automata; here one mostly sees a single actor, the Hamletperformer, speaking from a world of mechanical ruins.

The descriptions above are metaphorical because no single rational interpretation can be given of the effects of non-verbal performance on verbal performance. Again, even when the rendition of the text begins, many things continue to happen on stage which cannot but have a bearing on how the audience interprets the words and the whole. One aspect of the French translation which is absent from Wilson's, for instance, is that the barriers between the stage and the audience are partly torn down. During the fourth part of the performance, the main actor is followed by a spotlight as he pelts the stage with rock-like missiles from beside the stalls. Whether this particular moment reminds one more of Iron Curtain forms of surveillance (Kolpakova, Gataullina and Smyslova 2019) or twenty-first-century manifestations of public protest may depend on one's age and background; what is highly probable is that the directing choices here will make the audience feel insecure and threatened, and at the same time create some kind of identification with the Hamletperformer.

Another aspect of this production which makes it markedly different from Wilson's can be guessed from the number of times the term 'Hamletperformer' has been repeated in the last few paragraphs. Whereas in the 1986 American production the text is parcelled out among the cast, here it is spoken by a single actor – and when other actors do speak, their words are 'their own', in the sense that they are not taken from Müller's *Hamletmaschine*. In acting terms, this choice makes the whole production look more traditional: even if it is not always clear what the central actor is speaking about, there *is* a central actor, and his actions, appearance, demeanour and tone of voice give a sort of psychological unity to the whole that is completely absent in Wilson's assembly-line rendition. Entrusted with the task of reciting all of it from beginning to end, the Hamletperformer ends up tapping a variety of emotions that make the text stand out from its scrappy mechanized background like a piece of occult poetry spoken after a terrible disaster. In the end, although this version postpones the commencement of the text even more than Wilson's, it appears to do so out of respect, in order to create an effect of portentousness.

Whatever judgement one makes about these two productions as theatre translations, it is evident that in both cases it is clearly the intersemiotic element that has the greatest impact on what audiences experience. Obviously, interlingual translation is still necessary, since one production is in English and the other is in French; and as seen in the more recent version, some small intralingual adjustments may be put in place during performance, either by dropping some words or by adding lines which are external to Müller's text. Nevertheless, even though three levels of theatre translation are in play for Wilson's production and four for David Mambouch and Philippe Vincent's, the most important choices made by these directors and their collaborators clearly lie in the intersemiotic domain – in how they choose to frame the text in their complex theatrical machines.

8.3 *Translation in performance: Señor Serrano's* Birdie

Recently, experimental productions have tended to rely more and more consistently on the simultaneous deployment of several media and technologies. Of course, the theatre – even in its most mainstream incarnations – started incorporating cinema, music, radio and television almost as soon as it became possible to use them on stage. The last few decades, however, have seen a flowering of shows in which extraneous media have been put at the very centre of performance, with or without the participation of the audience: actors move and speak while their bodies are projected on a screen, and their utterances are recorded in real time, modified and relayed by loudspeakers; members of the audience are asked to answer personal questions related to the theme of the performance, and their answers are then shown on a large video display and made to become part of the scenography (Cerratto-Pargman, Rossitto and Barkhuus 2014: 608).

The interest of these kinds of performance for Translation Studies is twofold. On the one hand, in terms of interlingual translation, they often mix messages in different tongues (with English being employed to make the production as international as possible) as well as different modes (written and spoken). On the other, in terms of intersemiotic translation, they enact a communication between disparate media, both live and pre-recorded. Translation, in other words, becomes part of the theatrical experience itself, rather than just its preparation.

One production that is rich in interpretive possibilities in this sense is *Birdie*, a multimedia show created and first performed in 2016 by Catalan company Agrupación Señor Serrano and still touring worldwide. The title has a dual meaning, 'birdie' signifying a small bird but also a hole of golf completed with one stroke under the par. The show mixes the themes of human and animal migration and displacement with references to Hitchcock's *The Birds* and myriad other facets of contemporary life. Its unifying element is a picture taken by Melilla-based photographer José Palazón on 22 October 2014, showing a group of golfers who keep on playing while migrants are perching precariously on the high wall delimiting their green. Melilla being a Spanish enclave in Morocco, these bird-like figures are trying to cross the barrier dividing them from a world of real or imagined prosperity. The performance opens in Palazón's bedroom, at the moment of his waking, on the day that will see him take that photograph.

The last sentence in the above paragraph is somewhat misleading because it creates the impression of a fourth-wall, mimetic representation of life with a domestic setting and an actor moving within it. In this case, however, there is no conventional acting and there are no domestic scenes in any traditional sense. The protagonist's actions are narrated by a female voice in English, while two male performers create a sort of live installation: one of them stands on one side of a desk arranging various objects, and the other films those objects, which are projected onto a large screen and used as illustrations of what the female voice is saying (see Figure 5; the 'first cigarette of the day', for instance, is illustrated by a lit cigarette and a full ashtray). Apart from the objects filmed in real time, the screen shows surtitles bearing the same words as the female narrator is uttering – and whenever the narrator is not speaking, English surtitles are shown for any written messages that appear on screen in any language other than English.[6]

Even before that initial 'scene', the opening credits have given the audience a taste of the multimodal and translational nature of the piece. Much as if this were a film rather than a theatrical performance, its title is projected in reverse white type on a black screen, in elegant cursive script, with birdsong as a soundtrack. Immediately afterwards, the two relevant meanings of the term are explained in Catalan and English – a double act of intra- and interlingual

Figure 5 Live performance in *Birdie*. Photograph by Pasqual Gorriz. Courtesy of Agrupación Señor Serrano.

translation. Here is an approximate representation of how the translated dictionary definitions appear – again, in reverse white type on a black screen:

1. (Informal) A small bird.
2. (Sports) One stroke under par for a hole in golf.

1. (Informal) En anglès, ocellet.
2. (Esport) En el golf, un cop per sota del par.

The workings of the piece, however, are much more complex than that sample shows, integrating as they do intralingual, interlingual and intersemiotic translation. It is sufficient to describe six minutes of performance to bear witness to the incredible multiplicity of ways in which meanings are created, suggested, transferred from one language, one mode and one code to others. Between 2.45 and 8.30 mins, a single continuous scene is perceived as unfolding, as we are told that Palazón is having a shower (we hear the appropriate sounds, as well as a soul love song called 'Jose's soul', created by the company) and the two live performers show the pages of a Spanish newspaper (*El País* of 20 October 2014 – two days before the photograph is taken) on which they also superimpose extraneous photographs and transparencies. This continuous flow of projected images and words can be split into ten discrete descriptions.

1. (2.45–3.20 mins) A page of the newspaper is shown in which an article bearing the headline 'Treinta nuevos desplazados en el mundo cada minuto' ('Every minute, 30 people become displaced worldwide', in the terse surtitle translation) is illustrated by a stock photograph of an immense procession of people. A translated sub-heading gives more detailed information ('The number of displaced people rises up to 59.5 million'), while the camera moves down to frame a map of the world printed on the newspaper page, on which the performer not holding the camera superimposes a transparency with arrow-like vectors (Baldry and Thibault 2006: 35) detailing the human movements referred to in the headline, and with red circles foregrounding the final destinations to which most displaced persons aspire ('N. America'/'Europe'; see Kress and van Leeuwen (2006: 177) for the concept of 'salience'). Finally, a photograph showing rows on rows of tents is superimposed on the one on the *País* page, confirming the themes of migration, displacement and precarious human habitation.

2. (3.21–4.16 mins) Another page is turned. A photograph of a person in an oxygen tent, surrounded by standing people (doctors and nurses, one assumes), is shown on screen. The camera slowly moves down the page to reveal the headline 'Teresa Romero, curada tras dos semanas en el hospital' ('Teresa Romero, cured after two weeks in hospital'). The audience are informed by a sub-heading that the sick woman, too, is a nurse. Then the photograph of a smiling woman in a sweater is superimposed on the first picture, and one tends to identify this person as Romero herself, in her healthy state. The camera moves down again to frame a shorter article with a headline in smaller type: 'Excalibur, la cara triste del caso' – this translates literally as 'Excalibur, the sad face/side of the case', but is glossed by a more emotional surtitle which reads 'The slaughter of Excalibur, her dog, the sad aspect of the case' (Bednarek 2008: 11). One assumes that the animal had to be put down because it was contagious, and the assumption is strengthened by what follows. A map of Europe, the Near East and northern Africa is spread across the newspaper page: one slip of paper bearing the number '1' is put on Europe, another bearing the number '30,000' is put on Africa. Another translated heading informs the audience that 'The nurse was the first Ebola case in Europe.' The juxtaposition of these images and wordings, together with the affect used in the translation of the sub-heading about the dog, appears to show that a significant contrast is being presented between the general neglect with which the masses of non-European migrants in (1) are treated, and the great care dedicated to one European person infected with a sickness that killed 30,000 people in Africa.

3. (4.17–4.46 mins) On another page of the newspaper, a big headline reads 'La niña virtual "Sweetie" captura más de mil pedófilos on line', translated closely in the surtitle 'Girl avatar "Sweetie" catches more than 1,000 online paedophiles'. The camera moves up, and the audience see two photographs: on the left-hand side of the page, the dark silhouette of a man seated before a laptop, his head slightly bent towards the screen; on the right-hand side, the face of a girl in her early teens, presumably 'Sweetie'. That last assumption is confirmed when two further photographs are superimposed on the latter which show a girl-like figure with similar features, but eyes and complexion progressively more dehumanized and robot-like. Immediately afterwards, a transparency bearing vertical black lines is superimposed on the dark silhouette of the man. In this manner, an icon-like image is further iconized

(Machin 2009: 182–3) – i.e. made to represent one single concept: a man put behind bars because of his shady behaviour. The effect of clarification brought about by the intersemiotic translation of images into wordings (and vice versa) is heightened in this case by adding iconic aspects to the pictures.

4. (4.47–5.39 mins) The map of the world seen in (1) is shown again, but this time a different interpretation (intrasemiotic translation) is imposed on it in the shape of a transparency headed 'Línea mitocondrial', with arrow-like vectors taking off from East Africa to reach all regions of the world. Those members of the audience who can recall the initial appearance of that map, and automatically associate Africa with the idea of migrants, may perceive this as some sort of comment on the fact that the aboriginal home of most humans has been forsaken by its children. This hypothesis is confirmed by another newspaper headline: 'Un nuevo estudio confirma la existencia de una madre mitocondrial de todos los humanos' ('A new study confirms the existence of a mitochondrial mother of all living humans'). The addition of 'living' may be meant to remind the audience that they, too, share that ancestry: what is certain is that the presentation of a map of the world, as well as the parallels with previous sequences, confers an interpretive slant on a newspaper headline which would otherwise sound coolly scientific. Further confirmation that this may have been the theatre company's intention comes when the camera moves up to show a photograph of ancient fertility statuettes, then back down to shoot a new half-page bearing the headline 'Todos los seres humanos compartímos material genético de una mujer nacida en África Oriental hace 200.000 años'. This is translated very closely as 'All humans share genetic material from a woman born about 200,000 years ago in East Africa': interestingly, the typically Spanish inclusive we-form of the verb ('compartímos' – 'we share', coming after 'All human beings') is lost in this case – an interlingual modification which makes the heading more neutral and generic for the English monolingual reader.

5. (5.40–5.59 mins) This is a short interlude, showing various ads (presumably in the original newspaper) which can be seen to have more or less tenuous thematic and metaphorical links to the whole. An ad for golf balls bears a relation to both meanings of 'Birdie' expounded at the start: the ball has been turned into a visual pun by being placed in a bird's nest, while the whole is captioned with the words 'Born to fly'. Another ad is shown for

the (now defunct) American chain of toy retailers ToysЯUs, featuring action figures from the TV series *Breaking Bad* and the video-game franchise *Angry Birds*. No iconic explanation/verbal translation is given for these ads, and the audience are left to work out for themselves how golf balls in bird's nests, toys, breaking, badness, anger and angry birds are connected with the rest of the performance.

6. (6.00–6.32 mins) The related semantic fields of flying and migration are mined again, and connected with another aspect of human life. On screen, a photograph is shown of a row of trucks bearing the insignia of a gas and oil company – which, incidentally, bears the name of the external casing of a bird's egg. The headline above the picture reads: 'El flujo de capitales aumentará globalmente en 2015' ('Overall increase of capital flow in 2015'). A couple of sub-headings are shown, then the map of the world is newly superimposed on the newspaper page as the camera moves down. This time, the performer not holding the camera pairs the map with a transparency detailing the worldwide movements (migrations?) of oil. A few American and Chinese banknotes are then spread on the map.

7. (6.33–6.57 mins) One wonders briefly whether the banknotes, too, should be seen like birds, or wings, flying against the wind of oil flow – and then another page is turned and the camera focuses on a photograph of flying swifts. The headline that is projected immediately afterwards reads 'El vencejo común inicia su migración austral' ('The common swift begins its seasonal migration south'). The camera moves up, and the map of the world is seen once again. This time, the transparency details the migratory movements of this species.

8. (6.58–7.29 mins) There appears, filling the screen, a photograph of a woman in evening dress, holding a bottle of champagne. The bottle has just been opened, and the wine is shooting up over the woman's head to an impossible height and falling back down into a glass perched on her protruding backside. The camera moves down to frame a headline reading 'Kim Kardashian agradece las felicitaciones de cumpleaños' ('[Celebrity] Kim Kardashian grateful for her birthday wishes'). At this stage, many members of the audience will work out the implications of juxtaposing another image of Western superfluity with the stories of displaced humans and migrating birds. The multimodal metaphorical connection, however, runs deeper than

that, because at this point a piece of paper with a blue bird icon printed on a white background is thrown on the page. Kardashian's gratitude has evidently been expressed via the social medium 'Twitter'. Another slip of paper appears, on which her very tweet, complete with the emotive overflowing of that communication form (five exclamation marks at the end of the first sentence, the 'emojis' of a heart and a birthday cake at the end of the second), has been printed out. One of the performers throws a handful of confetti on the page.

9. (7.30–8.01 mins) Another page is turned, and a picture of a blonde woman looking into the camera fills the screen. The woman has a large crow perched on her right elbow. The camera moves up, and the headline '50 aniversario del estreno del film' ('50th anniversary of the film's Premiere') is seen, along with the words 'Tippi Hedren, Actriz' on the top left-hand side of the newspaper page. Then another photograph is superimposed on the first one, and the audience see an older blonde woman in a similar pose (but different dress), again with a crow on her elbow. Although no explicit indication is given, a lot of onlookers will recognize the allusions to Alfred Hitchcock's 1963 horror film *The Birds*. The camera then frames a sub-heading with a quote ('Los pájaros no existen, son nuestros propios miedos' / 'The birds doesn't [*sic*] exist, they're our own fears') which remains unattributed. Uncharacteristically, the camera lingers on this sub-heading for seven seconds, probably causing part of the audience to identify it as salient. Since the migrants in Palazón's picture will later be presented as birds, an early connection is established between perching creatures and 'our own fears'.

10. (8.02–8.30 mins) This time, the first thing that is seen is a sub-heading, translated by the surtitle 'They base their claim principally on the 16th-century fortress and the Art Nouveau heritage, second most important in Spain [*sic*].' As the camera moves up, the photograph of a harbour is seen (again, the semantic field of travelling is mined). Finally, the main headline is framed by the camera, and the article is thus revealed to be about Melilla, the setting of *Birdie*. Interestingly, the English surtitle glossing the Spanish headline 'Melilla presenta su candidatura para ser Patrimonio de la Humanidad' turns into '*The Spanish city of* Melilla presents its candidacy to become a UNESCO World Heritage Site' (italics mine). Since much of the show revolves around a contrast between impoverished African countries and Western opulence, one notes the significance of calling Melilla, a European enclave in Africa, a 'Spanish city'.

Though no single, all-encompassing interpretation can be imposed on this flow of wordings and images,[7] there is no doubt that some kind of thematic coherence is intended by its creators. *Birdie* is an open work, in the sense that no overt reading of its parts is imposed by the female narrator or any other authoritative figure. Nevertheless, it is not open in the same way as Müller's *Hamletmaschine*: it is not, that is, a modernist sum of parts meant to create free associations in the audience. The unifying theme of displacement is announced by the title itself and illustrated by Palazón's photograph. Once that central motif is established, given the contextual knowledge of a grown-up twenty-first-century onlooker, most of the words, sounds and images of the show end up taking a certain slant. As explained by its promotional presentation (which is much more explicit than the show), *Birdie* contrasts a world of 'war, drought, massive deforestation' with one of 'supermarkets, safe streets, family and stability', and its ostensive aim is to lead audiences to ask themselves questions about 'the use of building walls against flocks of birds'.[8]

What is of interest in the present context, however, is not how open or ideologically charged this work is, but how much the associations it stimulates in the audience depend on the four levels of theatre translation. In the presentation of the title, the creators use intralingual translation (a dictionary definition) to outline the contrast they will then explore between opulence (people playing golf) and poverty (the migrants as bird-like figures). In the sequence analysed above, intersemiotic translation is used throughout in order to illustrate wordings or define the otherwise vague meanings of images: a headline about migrants is furnished with a photograph turning numbers into human beings, while a sub-heading about birds as the embodiment of 'our' fears is also shown on screen. The element of intrasemiotic translation, though less evident, must also be taken into account: the various transparencies superimposed on the map of the world, for instance, create semantic connections between birds and humans, the migration of refugees and the common origins of all women and men. Finally, interlingual translation is everywhere in the continuous operation of English surtitling – and it becomes meaningful when there is a perceptible lexicogrammatical gap between source and target wordings: when the death of the nurse's dog is explained and lamented in the surtitles of (2), or when Melilla is defined as a Spanish city in those of (10), some or most viewers will link the additional feelings and information to the sum of related meanings activated by the sequence, and by *Birdie* as a whole theatre act.

8.4 Conclusion: Performance-centric theatre and the resistance of text

Works like those presented above may fall, in certain European theatrical milieux, under the common capacious umbrella of 'experimental' or 'contemporary' theatre – but they are, of course, quite distinct in origin, conception and realization. Heiner Müller's *Hamletmaschine* is originally a modernist (or postmodern) freely associating text with strong political overtones, stemming from a country behind the Iron Curtain in the late 1970s. In the decades following its composition, before and after its author's death, it has been presented by a great number of directors in a great variety of manners. *Birdie*, by contrast, looks much more like a typical product of the third millennium: it does not originate in text, but directly as a multimedia production mixing live performances, live filming and a pre-recorded soundtrack. *Die Hamletmaschine* can become *Hamletmachine*, *La macchina Amleto* or *Máquina Hamlet*, and each of its intralingual or interlingual productions will be different from all others. *Birdie* is just *Birdie*: small differences in execution will arise from one show to the next, but only because the timing of the performers will change slightly. Therefore, only Heiner Müller's work can be analysed in terms of theatre translation, as those terms have been defined in the present monograph; but Agrupación Señor Serrano's multimedia realization is still very interesting in terms of Theatrical Translation Studies, as it illustrates a growing tendency to employ translation live on stage.

The unifying aspect of these two works, however – the reason why they have been brought together in this chapter – is that neither can be understood by reference to words alone. Of course, even *Il pastor fido* was performed in the context of lavish mises-en-scène whose details are now mostly lost to us, and such contemporary but more traditional works as the French or Italian versions of *The Secretary Bird* depend on actors and scenography for their effects. But while Guarini's and Douglas Home's plays tell stories that can

be summarized in the same way as the story told by any of their theatrical/
cinematic translations, describing a performance of *Die Hamletmaschine* or
Birdie means gauging the combined effect of language and other codes. Heiner
Müller's text exists as a separate entity, but no one would be able to read it and
imagine the details of any of its productions; and one could think of rendering
all of *Birdie* as in the above description, but the effect would be very different
from witnessing *Birdie* as performed by Agrupación Señor Serrano. Because
they share this quality, both works are useful in demonstrating that linguistic
analysis is not enough to understand what happens in theatre translation, or
generally in theatre performance. Again, this is as true for twentieth-century
word-centric theatre as it is for any postmodern experimental production –
but in the latter case, very little is left when the inter- and intrasemiotic levels
of theatre translation are taken out of the equation.

In conclusion, and partly in contrast with what has been said so far, it
is worth mentioning that there are occasions – even within the capacious
category of experimental, performance-centric theatre – on which something
does remain when those levels are left out: and it is fascinating to see how that
something, when it exists, tends to concentrate the attention of a cultural and
academic world which is still very much text-centric in many of its habits.
As seen above, *Die Hamletmaschine* was born as a piece of writing before an
actual performance was even imagined – and while it spawned a multiplicity of
interpretive productions, it was written by a playwright who, two years before,
had opined that 'it's literature's job to resist the theatre' (Barnett 2016: 19).[9]
If it is impossible to gauge the success with which Müller's play has 'resisted'
all its stage realizations, it is possible to note two text-centric results of this
attitude: on the one hand, while Müller's stage directions have been used in
imaginative ways, his lines of monologue have mostly been kept intact; on the
other, the text itself has been published in all European languages, in isolation
and in authoritative collections of its author's works. Since the process of
Müller's canonization began before his death, this is, of course, inevitable, the
publication of all works of an author being part of that process. But in the case
of *Die Hamletmaschine*, it is significant that textual editions and translations of
that work alone have also been published (see Keim 1998;[10] Müller 1995, 2003,
2012), and that some of those editions have been accompanied by the scholarly
apparatus that marks off great works of literature from the dross of everyday

reading. One wonders what would happen to a multimedia production like *Birdie* if it ended up acquiring canonical status – if, in other words, the need was felt to preserve it for future generations. Would people be content with a filmed version of the performance being uploaded online? Or would it become necessary to produce some paper testimony of its existence?

Conclusion: What this book is not about

At least in its inception, this book was conceived in much the same way as a medieval *Summa*: not so much an original contribution as a recapitulation of what is already there, which only needs to be teased out and clarified. If one looks at the panorama of theatrical translation theory through the ages and in the last six decades, one sees that everything, and the opposite of everything, has already been said. Most writers have treated theatre translation as an essentially textual phenomenon, but some have concentrated on performance to the detriment of text; certain theorists have observed the whole process in terms of despairing complication, but others have exulted at the layered richness of the experience; most have considered that process from the translator's point of view, but a few have attempted to analyse it from above or from a distance. *Theatre Translation* is an attempt at subsuming all these approaches (Part I), unifying them into a single methodology (Part II) and applying that methodology to the analysis of a variety of case studies (Part III).

Inevitably, it is not a neutral attempt: its ideological slant is denounced by its very title and declared in Part II, but it also informs the theoretical survey of Part I and the analyses of Part III – in both cases, with a clear progression from text- to performance-centric approaches and productions. As well as the general organization of the book, this underlying ideology has guided the selection of theoretical materials and case studies. A number of theories have been left out or given bare mentions in Part I, not because they are not valid, but because they do not amount to theoretical advancements in terms of the progression identified above. Analogously, in Part III, only a handful of very different theatre genres and translation forms have been chosen out of an immense variety of possibilities, in the interests of elucidation and argument. After all, as medieval scholars must have known, no *Summa* is a bare, or even (paradoxically) a complete, summation. So, to rephrase the beginning of this conclusion: this book is a recapitulation of what is already there, but in the process, 'what is already there' gets sifted and organized in personal ways and is deployed for a certain overall purpose.

The overall purpose is needed to give point, coherence and cohesion to the whole, and keep the book down to a manageable size: but it entails cuts and simplifications which may often feel painful – for the writer as well as for the specialized reader. In Part I, many sections and even single paragraphs could be expanded into whole monographs – and fortunately, some of them have been, by scholars whose work is mentioned and included in the list of references. To give just a few examples, Plautus and Terence should be studied in the context of the wider tradition of Roman writing and translating. The story of how Shakespeare invaded the book markets and national theatres of Europe has just been touched upon here, as has the relationship between German Romanticism and translated theatre/drama. The entire tradition of French theatre translation is reduced to a few chance comments on Ducis. The whole discipline of Theatre Studies, with its contributions on the topic of theatre translation, might call for a much broader treatment.

The omissions in terms of case studies are even more glaring: three or four theatrical genres and a handful of texts/productions have been chosen to deputize for theatre traditions and translations of all kinds, at all times. *Il pastor fido* is only one of a great number of sixteenth-century Italian pastoral plays, which in themselves form only a part of the immense theatrical production of the Renaissance – and a discussion of three English translations does not even begin to exhaust the question of Guarini's impact on European poetry, drama and theatre. Two recent Italian productions certainly cannot be said to be representative of mainstream European theatre at large. *Die Hamletmaschine* and *Birdie* are just two (very different) examples of what 'experimental theatre' has come to mean in the last few decades. And what should one say of all the centuries of recorded drama and theatre which are left out altogether, or of all the translation cultures and traditions which barely get a mention?

Admittedly, some of these omissions are not only motivated by a need for selection but also consequent on the linguistic and academic limitations of this particular writer. An Italian identity and a grounding in English linguistics and literature mean that the bulk of examples are taken from two cultures, even though various efforts are made to widen the scope of the inquiry. Those efforts, however, are confined to the range of languages of which the writer has at least some working knowledge – Italian, English, Latin, French, German and Spanish. Russian, Finnish or Hungarian theatre, therefore, must remain out of the picture, as must any untranslated theory in any other language. Even more importantly, perhaps, the focus of the monograph is a European one, or at most a transatlantic one. Nothing is said about non-Western traditions and views, which may or may not fit into the terminology and methodology proposed here.

Ultimately, such failings are inevitable, and will have to be addressed by better researchers and/or by the whole academic community, which is always wiser than any of its representatives. As regards the theories and practices about which this book is silent, *Theatre Translation* is a shot in the dark. It is to be hoped that by a stroke of luck, that shot is accurate enough to be of use, as a guide, for anybody with a better aim.

Notes

Chapter 1

1 Naturally, Plautus and Terence share this comparatively libertine attitude to translation with most Roman writers and orators, and that attitude was greatly favoured by having to work with unwieldy scrolls which could hardly be conceived of as complete works. Siobhán McElduff (2013: 7–15) is very eloquent on the relationship between Roman thinking on translation and the existing technology of reading and writing. Similar things can be said on the connection between medieval translation freedom and manuscript culture. It was only with the humanists, when texts began to be considered as sacred, inviolable units (and even more when their status was consecrated by print), that a text-centric, source-oriented culture of translation was born.

2 On the ambiguity of 'vortit barbare', which lies somewhere between homage and mockery, see McElduff (2013, 66–78). Gilula (1989) notes that even on stage, Plautus' translations were probably apt to denounce themselves as such – thus momentarily destroying not only the audience's suspension of disbelief but also their illusion that they were watching something speaking directly to them, in their language and to their culture. Of course, this was also inherent in the nature of the *palliata*, in which actors wore Greek clothing and the scene was set in Greece.

3 See also Albini and Petrone (1992: 434–7). That Terence is also partly fretting about his uncertain status as author-translator is evident from the Prologue to *Eunuchus*, where the actor begs the audience to forgive modern poets if they do what ancient poets have already done – because, after all, there is nothing on earth that has not been said before ('nullum est iam dictum quod non dictum sit prius. / qua re aequom est vos cognoscere atque ignoscere / quae veteres factitarunt si faciunt novi'; Terentius 1989: 266).

4 Translation mine. Henceforth, all translations without a citation are to be attributed to the present author.

5 At least in the *Republican* Roman world: for Seneca's rather different treatment of his Greek sources, see Albini and Petrone (1992: 437, 642–68), McElduff (2013: 161–4).

6   Significantly, this was not often the case thereafter, particularly for Terence – who was seen in later ages, rightly or wrongly, as a slavish follower of his models. Bertini (1989: xxiii) notes, for instance, that in the first part of the twentieth century, while Plautus was praised as an original playwright, many classical scholars considered Terence to be 'merely' an elegant translator of Greek playbooks ('nulla più che un fine ed elegante traduttore di copioni greci').

7   In this volume, see especially Mullini 2016 on how the need for different 'translations', or at the very least presentations, of this biblical material might make itself felt in a changing, contentious religious landscape.

8   Of course, the appropriation of Seneca on stage (a form of unacknowledged translation) is quite a different matter (Winston 2006: 175).

9   Admittedly, most ancient and Renaissance plays are in verse: but what is meant here is that these treatises concentrate on their poetic value, at the expense of their theatrical effectiveness.

10 Helou (2003: 12) mentions the fact that Erasmus' Latin Euripides was used by university theatre troupes at Cambridge and Leuven.

11 This reference to syllables inevitably evokes the medieval and Renaissance debate on religious translation, with Jerome insisting on word order being a mystery in the Scriptures and the Protestant Miles Smith, many centuries later, asking polemically whether God's kingdom had 'become words or syllables' (The Bible 1997: lxviii). Evidently, Schlegel is treating Shakespeare as a 'sacred' canonical author.

12 See also Levý (2000: 154), where translations from Shakespeare and Molière are judged in terms of 'semantic' dispersion.

Chapter 2

1   Hermans (1999) provides a general historical overview of this diverse 'school' and a detailed discussion of the various labels that have been applied to it (Hermans himself opts for 'Polysystems Theory', a definition that foregrounds Itamar Even-Zohar's contribution).

2   Of course, this text-centric quality does not in any way detract from their importance. It is to be noted in passing that Toury's notion of norms has been adapted to the analysis of performance-centric genres (e.g. Karamitroglou 2000) – and that Venuti's later studies, while still largely focusing on text, are much more promising in terms of application to Theatrical Translation Studies.

The title itself of his 2013 collection of essays, *Translation Changes Everything*, illustrates this point.

3   Sirkku Aaltonen, whose work is presented extensively in the next chapter, has produced valuable works on theatrical 'acculturation', both in more text-centric terms (1996) and with a sociolinguistic focus on the audience (2020).

4   Zuber-Skerritt's linguistic bearings are slightly out of sync with the age: in 1983, the contributors to the Italian collection *Interazione, dialogo, convenzioni* (Aston 1983) had used the rising discipline of pragmatics as a more appropriate set of tools for analysing drama and theatre translation.

Chapter 3

1   Bourdieu's term 'cultural capital' will be used quite often in the 'practice' section. See Bourdieu (1984) and Lefevere (1998) for an application in the field of Translation Studies.

2   In her introduction to the 2013 monographic issue of *Target* discussed below, Cristina Marinetti quotes from an editorial by Charlotte Canning in which the latter points out that theatre is no longer confined by the physical limits of live rendition – 'it can be tweeted, texted, posted on YouTube, simulcast and delivered through a host of other electronic means' (Canning 2013: 2; Marinetti 2013a: 317).

3   In this sense, it is perhaps significant to note that the editors are at pains to point out that 'academic interest in translation in the context of drama and theatre has been flourishing well beyond translation studies, the traditional home of research on translation' (Baines, Marinetti and Perteghella 2011: 1) – as if they wanted to assert from the very beginning their independence of any of the theories developed within the discipline.

4   Though it must be noted, in passing, that some text-centric emphasis can still be detected in her seemingly performance-centric words. Questions must be asked about 'the force the text has in performance'.

5   To appreciate the performative angle of these monographs, a comparison with older studies such as Brisset (1990) is very useful.

6   See also Ambrosi 2013, in the same volume; or Alan J. E. Wolf in *Staging and Performing Translation*, when he opines that it is overly pessimistic to think that 'translations are irretrievably severed from the original text's intentions' (Wolf 2011: 102).

7 The reference to Newmark's production is particularly revealing, because in his textbooks of the 1980s this scholar maintains the same text-centric dichotomies that have been observed in Levý's and Mounin's monographs. For Newmark, 'when a play is transferred from the SL to the TL culture it is usually no longer a translation, but an adaptation' (Newmark 1988: 173).

8 A very striking example of text-centric and source-bound resistance is offered by the article on 'Theatre' in the 2019 *Routledge Handbook of Literary Translation*: recent theoretical developments are completely ignored, and the author opines that future translators might feel emboldened to preserve the signs of the 'Other', of the 'original', in their target texts (Racz 2019). It is also interesting to note that the resistance of text- and source-bound biases can be detected in historical surveys as well as translator-centred studies: Catherine O'Leary (2018: 59), for instance, notes that 'The gap between O'Casey's originals and Sastre's versions [...] raises the interesting question of responsibility to the original text and to the intention of the original author.'

Chapter 4

1 Though highly influential, of course, Artaud and Brecht were by no means the first to theorize or realize a form of distancing between page and stage. Artaud, for instance, was in turn influenced by surrealism, and dadaists also liked to play with theatrical conventions (see Bay-Cheng 2007).

2 Again, these examples of intercultural theatre from the late twentieth century were arguably preceded and influenced by the intercultural interests of such avant-garde and modernist authors as Artaud and W. B. Yeats (see Farfan and Knowles 2011). See the special issue of *Theatre Studies* edited by Farfan and Knowles (but also Bharucha 1993; Suvin 2001; Lee 2018) for a discussion of how the notion of intercultural theatre has ended up being criticized as colonial and hegemonic.

3 It is also interesting to note that this chapter was first published in 1989 as a contribution to a collection edited by Hanna Scolnicov and Peter Holland. *The Play Out of Context: Transferring Plays from Culture to Culture* was a fairly concerted attempt by a group of theatre scholars to study translation in cultural and performance-centric terms, as well as on the linguistic plane – or, to use Scolnicov's own words, to 'examine the relationship between the play and its historical and cultural contexts' (Scolnicov 1989: 1; see also Holland 1989).

4   See also Spencer (2007: 391): 'Contemporary theories of translation
    notwithstanding, theatre scholarship on translation has primarily focused on the
    transfer of scripts from one language to another, looking at a semiotic range from
    literal transcription to free adaptation, or on intercultural theatre practices in
    which issues of dominant language cannot be ignored.'

5   This is also true of more recent articles from the same line of research: see, for
    instance, Gindt (2013), which employs the notion of cultural translation with one
    single reference to Peter Burke.

Chapter 5

1   Of course, using the term 'performative function' here would create confusion
    with the distinction between 'text-' and 'performance-centric' approaches.

2   Unsurprisingly, the term can be found in the performance-centric writings of
    Pavis (1992), Bassnett (1998), Aaltonen (2000) and Marinetti (2013a), and in the
    very titles of Upton (2000) and Bigliazzi, Kofler and Ambrosi (2013).

3   Another popular term is 'rewriting': for a recent example, see the very interesting
    collection of views on Egyptian theatre in Aaltonen and Ibrahim (2016).

4   Even theorists who accept the inevitability of non-equivalence in the theatrical
    domain still – rather confusingly – use the term 'adaptation' to illustrate the
    transformative nature of theatre translation (see, for instance, Laera 2019:
    25–39).

5   There is actually no reason why Theatrical Translation Studies should not be able
    to apply its analytical tools to intralingual translations (e.g. English rewritings
    of Shakespeare's plays), but for the purposes of the present monograph and
    its analyses, the scope will be confined to transactions which comprehend
    interlingual translation.

6   The audience is also an influencing factor in the production of any theatre
    act – both when its contribution is actively requested, as in certain kinds of
    contemporary theatre, and when it is simply tolerated and reacted to, as happens
    in more traditional performative events. However, since it is extremely difficult
    to gauge the effects of audience participation, this aspect of performance will
    only be briefly touched upon here (see Bennett (1997) for a book-length study of
    the relation between production and spectatorship).

7   Jakobson's definition is here reprised and extended without any consideration for
    his approach, or for other updated versions of semiotic translation theory. For a
    recent overview and revision of these, see Jia (2017).

Chapter 6

1 See Guarini (1590), which bears a later date than that of its actual publication (December 1589; see Frodella 2012: 114).

2 Interestingly, the title page of this English edition kept the wedding dedication of the Venetian book – either because Wolfe and Castelvetro thought it added prestige to their book, or because they wanted to present it as if it were just another copy of the original publication.

3 The English play is also presented as a vindication of the qualities of northern, Germanic English. This is a view Daniel would articulate a year later in his brief *Defence of Ryme* (see Morini 2020b).

4 The choruses are also the only occasions on which Fanshawe departs from his pentameter line, though he continues writing in couplets. Dymock too, in 1602, had felt the need to apply variation: his choruses, like Guarini's, have rhyme and lines of varying length.

5 This theatre translation runs to a total of around 19,000 words, vs Dymock's 34,000 and the 46,000 of the Fanshawe translation on which it is based. The dialogue is shortened everywhere, and the choruses are excised.

Chapter 7

1 Barbareschi also confirmed, in the course of several interviews and press conferences, that he had personally worked on the English play in order to adapt it for contemporary Italian audiences. See, for instance, <https://www.youtube.com/watch?v=T_vtLEOkj3E> (accessed 18 June 2021).

2 While plays of this kind, by Douglas Home and others, have continued to be revived and still enjoy a degree of success abroad, it can be argued that in terms of theatre and literary history they were obscured by works produced in the same period by John Osborne, Arnold Wesker, Harold Pinter and others. See Stevenson 2004 (274–6) for an account of the hostility of influential figures such as Kenneth Tynan towards the comfortable settings and comforting plots of upper-class theatre. More recently, see Rousseau (2019a) for an account of Douglas Home as one of the best representatives of the lighter side of 1960s British drama.

3 Here and in the rest of the section, all the quotations from and descriptions of Barbareschi's *L'anatra all'arancia* are dependent on a performance televised by Rai in 2017, and retrievable at the following internet address: <https://www.

youtube.com/watch?v=45hr5xgnEPE&t=2794s> (last accessed 18 June 2021). Having been asked at the beginning of 2018 to introduce the play for theatre audiences in Forlì, I was also able to compare the dialogue here with a script sent to me by the company – but whenever the Italian play is quoted, the words are taken from its staged, televised version (always slightly different from the text).

4 'LISA: Guarda che quello lì è il miglior centro estetico di Milano. Poi fra l'altro meno male che avevo prenotato perché c'era pieno di gente, pieno. / GILBERTO: Ah sì? Pompieri, immagino. / LISA: Pompieri? Perché? / GILBERTO: C'è stato un incendio! / LISA: Un incendio? / GILBERTO: Sì, l'han detto in televisione. Ha bruciato tutto il palazzo sopra il centro estetico. Pensavo te ne fossi accorta – a meno che non pensassi che l'odore di bruciato erano i peli della ceretta. / LISA: Ci son state delle vittime? / GILBERTO: Una sola – eccola qui. (*Le porge il bicchiere*) / LISA: Oddio mi spiace. Guarda, mi spiace veramente, Gilberto. Io avrei dovuto raccontarti tutto tanto tempo fa. / GILBERTO: Non ti preoccupare. Io lavoro in televisione. É giusto che venga a sapere dalla televisione che sono cornuto. Chi è il vincitore? / LISA: Volodia. Volodia Smirnov.' (1.16–3.16 mins.)

5 The source title, in point of fact, is a pun on one of the characters in the play: Molly Forsyth is Hugh Walford's secretary, and she is presented as quite an attractive young woman (a 'bird'); but the 'secretary bird' is also an African bird of prey that feeds on snakes – thus, metaphorically, it is the ploy used by the husband to kill the viper in his bosom, his wife's lover. None of these possible meanings are reflected in the Italian title: in Italian, *oca* (goose) is used metaphorically to refer to a silly young woman, but no such meaning attaches to *anatra* (duck).

6 The use of the variant spelling *anitra* for *anatra* was probably due to the fact that Ibsen's *Vildanden* (*The Wild Duck*) was famous in Italy with the nineteenth-century title *L'anitra selvatica*.

7 <https://www.youtube.com/watch?v=gA2qbNwRtoA> (accessed 18 June 2021). As for the re-publication of Sauvajon's script (Douglas Home and Sauvajon 2019), it was occasioned by a new production created in 2018 for the Festival of Anjou. Give or take a few minor variations, the dialogue in these two versions is clearly the same, and the 2019 publication can therefore be considered to be a close reproduction of Sauvajon's script (as its editors claim).

8 The stage directions have been left out of the translated quotation. Here is the French text: 'LIZ: [...] L'incendie? ... / HUGH: Je pensais que tu l'avais remarqué. D'aprés la radio, il a fallu évacuer l'immeuble ... [...] Rassure-toi, il semble bien que je sois la seule victime! / [...] LIZ: Je suis navrée, Hugh ... J'aurais dû t'avouer tout ça depuis déjà mal de temps mais ... / HUGH: Je travaille à la BBC, chérie. Il

est tout à fait normal que ce soit la radio qui m'ait appris que je suis cocu … […]
Il s'appelle comment, le gagnant? […] LIZ: […] John Brownlow.' (Douglas Home
and Sauvajon 2019: 15.)

9   'Marc-Gilbert Sauvajon, artiste aux multiples talents, semble approcher les textes
    anglais qu'il a l'habitude de côtoyer à la manière dì un auteur plutôt que d'un
    traducteur' (Rousseau 2019b: 95).

10 See, for instance, this translation (again, from 'Two Acts by W.D. Home and
    M.A. [*sic*] Sauvajon' attributed to 'Francesco Orsini'): <https://www.ateatro.info/
    copioni/lanatra-allarancia/> (accessed 18 June 2021).

11 Retrievable online at <https://www.youtube.com/watch?v=fhTpN0bsJ08&t=56s>
    (accessed 18 June 2021).

12 An omission which was replicated in most of the available reviews of
    the production. See, for instance, <https://www.lastampa.it/milano/
    appuntamenti/2017/11/12/news/la-guerra-dei-roses-crudele-eppure-
    comica-1.34383659> (accessed 18 June 2021) or <https://www.teatro.it/
    recensioni/la-guerra-dei-roses/la-guerra-dei-roses-o-piuttosto-la-battaglia-dei-
    sessi> (accessed 18 June 2021).

13 The references to the English play contain indications of acts and scenes rather
    than pages, because it was published in its original form, in 2008, as an e-book.
    As for the Italian production, I saw it twice – on 22 and 24 November 2018. The
    script was very close to the English play, with minor differences in the religious
    puns and references which could be explained in terms of cultural translation.
    As regards the textual translation, it was attributed in all promotional material
    to Antonia Brancati and Enrico Luttmann, but it is perfectly possible that the
    2016 stage production as it is described in this chapter was the outcome of a sum
    of forces – more specifically, of the producers, director and actors modifying an
    initial interlingual version on the intralingual and intersemiotic planes.

14 It is interesting to note that in an evident attempt to adapt the original plot
    (retrospectively) to the film, the protagonist of the twentieth-anniversary version
    of the novel is called Oliver (Adler 2001). Confusingly, though, Adler retained
    'Jonathan' for the 2008 play.

Chapter 8

1   Various practitioners and theorists have seen the modern translation of Greek
    plays in a very similar light to the translation and production of contemporary

'experimental' theatre – the source texts are often so incomplete, and express such a remote culture, that the only road to success is dramatic and performative reinterpretation (Mee 2007; Wiles 2007). Something very similar can be said for Eastern productions of Western texts (Liu 2007), as well as the expensive 'intercultural' Western interpretations of 'other' cultures (with, in this case, heavier post-colonial political implications; see Lei (2011), who looks at Robert Wilson's work in terms of cultural appropriation; and O'Toole 2013).

2   Gordon Rogoff (1986: 55) called the text 'an artifact waiting for a director'.

3   Different accounts (Rogoff 1986: 55; Barnett 2016: 50) give different numbers – possibly reflecting different performances.

4   The Lyon performance is visible at <https://www.youtube.com/watch?v=qA01eT-uyDs> (40.32 mins; accessed 18 June 2021). Henceforth, all references will be to this mise-en-scène.

5   The translation is attributed to Jean Jourdheuil and Heinz Schwarzinger, whose printed French translation of Müller's working papers contains the missing words, as well as a lot of material expunged in the final version of the text (Müller 2003).

6   In a performance for the Ipercorpo Festival in Forlì (1 June 2019), Italian subtitles were projected for all English surtitles in the piece. The performance described below was first seen at a Catalan festival (I was able to watch it by means of a private link generously provided by the company).

7   To simplify the analysis, the impact of the soundtrack (the song with its rhythm, its mood, its lyrics for English-speaking listeners; the sound of the shower Palazón is taking) has been excluded from the detailed description. On the variety of effects that music can have on listeners, in particular, see Van Leeuwen (1999) and Morini (2013c).

8   Quoted from <https://www.srserrano.com/it/birdie/> (accessed 18 June 2021).

9   Unsurprisingly, Müller expressed his appreciation for Wilson's faithfulness to his words: 'The text says what it says […] Wilson never interprets: that is a very important quality, and I find it interesting. Here is a text, and it is delivered, but it never gets evaluated, coloured or interpreted' ['Was der Text sagt, sagt der Text […] Wilson interpretiert nie, und das finde ich eine ganz wesentliche Qualität, und das interessiert mich. Da ist ein Text, und der wird abgeliefert, aber nicht bewertet und nicht gefärbt und nicht interpretiert'] (Müller 2014: 54).

10   The very book which is used in this chapter as source for *Die Hamletmaschine* pairs Müller's text with a collection of essays on its theatrical, literary, philosophical and political significance.

References

Aaltonen, Sirkku (1996), *Acculturation of the Other: Irish Milieux in Finnish Drama Translation*, Joensuu: University of Joensuu Publications in the Humanities.

Aaltonen, Sirkku (1997), 'Translating Plays or Baking Apple Pies: A Functional Approach to the Study of Drama Translation', in Mary Snell-Hornby, Zuzana Jettmarová, Klaus Kaindl (eds), *Translation as Intercultural Communication: Selected Papers from the EST Congress – Prague 1995*, 89–97, Amsterdam: John Benjamins.

Aaltonen, Sirkku (2000), *Time-Sharing on Stage: Drama Translation in Theatre and Society*, Clevedon: Multilingual Matters Ltd.

Aaltonen, Sirkku (2013), 'Theatre Translation *as Performance*', *Target*, 25 (3): 385–406.

Aaltonen, Sirkku (2020), *Code-Choice and Identity Construction on Stage*, London: Routledge.

Aaltonen, Sirkku, and Areeg Ibrahim, eds (2016), *Rewriting Narratives in Egyptian Theatre: Translation, Performance, Politics*, London: Routledge.

Adler, Warren (1981), *The War of the Roses*, New York: Warner Books.

Adler, Warren (2001), *The War of the Roses*, New York: Stonehouse Productions.

Adler, Warren (2008), *The War of the Roses: The Play*, New York: Stonehouse Productions.

Albini, Umberto, and Gianna Petrone (1992), *Storia del Teatro: I Greci – I Romani*, Milano: Garzanti.

Ambrosi, Paola (2013), 'Verse Translation for the Theatre: A Spanish Example', in Silvia Bigliazzi, Peter Kofler and Paola Ambrosi (eds), *Theatre Translation in Performance*, 61–76, New York: Routledge.

Anderman, Gunilla (2005), *Europe on Stage: Translation and Theatre*, London: Oberon Books.

Andrews, Richard (1993), *Scripts and Scenarios: The Performance of Comedy in Renaissance Italy*, Cambridge: Cambridge University Press.

Andrews, Richard (2014), 'Shakespeare and Italian Comedy', in Andrew Hadfield and Paul Hammond (eds), *Shakespeare and Renaissance Europe*, 123–49, London: Bloomsbury.

Asimov, Isaac (1941), 'Nightfall', *Astounding Science Fiction*, 28 (1): 9–34.

Assis Rosa, Alexandra, Hanna Pięta and Rita Bueno Maia (2017), 'Theoretical, Methodological and Terminological Issues Regarding Indirect Translation: An Overview', *Translation Studies*, 10 (2): 113–32.

Aston, Guy et al. (1983), *Interazione, dialogo, convenzioni: Il caso del testo drammatico*, Bologna: CLUEB.

Austin, J. L. (1962), *How to Do Things with Words*, Oxford: Oxford University Press.

Baines, Roger, and Fred Dalmasso (2011), 'Musical Realizations: A Performance-based Translation of Rhythm in Koltès' *Dans la solitude des champs de coton*', in Roger Baines, Cristina Marinetti and Manuela Perteghella (eds), *Staging and Performing Translation: Text and Theatre Practice*, 49–71, Houndmills, Basingstoke: Palgrave Macmillan.

Baines, Roger, and Manuela Perteghella (2011), 'Interview with Christopher Hampton', in Roger Baines, Cristina Marinetti and Manuela Perteghella (eds), *Staging and Performing Translation: Text and Theatre Practice*, 173–86, Houndmills, Basingstoke: Palgrave Macmillan.

Baines, Roger, Cristina Marinetti and Manuela Perteghella (2011), 'Introduction', in Roger Baines, Cristina Marinetti and Manuela Perteghella (eds), *Staging and Performing Translation: Text and Theatre Practice*, 1–8, Houndmills, Basingstoke: Palgrave Macmillan.

Baldry, Anthony, and P. J. Thibault (2006), *Multimodal Transcription and Text Analysis*, London: Equinox.

Bantinaki, Katerina (2020), 'The Literary Translator as Author: A Philosophical Assessment of the Idea', *Translation Studies*, 13 (3): 306–17.

Barnett, David (2014), 'Heiner Müller, *Die Hamletmaschine*', in Peter W. Marx (ed.), *Hamlet-Handbuch: Stoffe, Aneignungen, Deutungen*, 422–8, Stuttgart: Metzler.

Barnett, David (2016), *Heiner Müller's* The Hamletmachine, London: Routledge.

Bassnett, Susan (1980), 'An Introduction to Theatre Semiotics', *Theatre Quarterly*, 10 (38): 47–55.

Bassnett, Susan (1981), 'The Problems of Translating Theatre Texts', *Theatre Quarterly*, 10 (40): 37–49.

Bassnett, Susan (1983), 'Problemi della traduzione di testi teatrali', in Guy Aston et al., *Interazione, dialogo, convenzioni: Il caso del testo drammatico*, 49–61, Bologna: CLUEB.

Bassnett, Susan (1985), 'Ways through the Labyrinth: Strategies and Methods for Translating Theatre Texts', in Theo Hermans (ed.), *The Manipulation of Literature*, 97–103, London: Croom Helm.

Bassnett, Susan (1990), 'Translating for the Theatre: Textual Complexities', *Essays in Poetics*, 15 (1): 71–84.

Bassnett, Susan (1998), 'Still Trapped in the Labyrinth: Further Reflections on Translation and Theatre', in Susan Bassnett and André Lefevere, *Constructing Cultures*, 90–108, Clevedon: Multilingual Matters.

Bassnett, Susan (2002), *Translation Studies*, 3rd edn, London: Routledge.

Bassnett, Susan, and Peter Bush, eds (2006), *The Translator as Writer*, London: Continuum.

Bassnett, Susan, and André Lefevere, eds (1990), *Translation, History & Culture*, London: Pinter.

Basso, Susanna (2010), *Sul tradurre: Esperienze e divagazioni militanti*, Milano: Bruno Mondadori.

Bauer, Wolfgang (1999), 'The Role of Intermediate Languages in Translations from Chinese into German', in Viviane Alleton and Michael Lackner (eds), *De L'un au multiple. Traduction du chinois vers les langues européennes. Translation from Chinese into European Languages*, 19–32, Paris: Éditions de la Maison des sciences de l'homme.

Bay-Cheng, Sarah (2007), 'Typography, and the Avant-Garde's Impossible Text', *Theatre Journal*, 59 (3): 467–83.

Bednarek, Monika (2008), *Emotion Talk across Corpora*, Houndmills, Basingstoke: Palgrave Macmillan.

Belingard, Laurence (2017), 'Traduire, créer', *Meta* 62 (3): 489–500.

Benjamin, Walter (1961), *Illuminationen: Ausgewählte Schriften*, Berlin: Suhrkamp.

Bennett, Susan (1997), *Theatre Audiences: A Theory of Production and Reception*, 2nd edn, London: Routledge.

Bertini, Ferruccio (1989), 'Terenzio e la critica letteraria', in Publius Afer Terentius, *Le commedie*, xviii–xxvii, Milano: Garzanti.

Bharucha, Rustom (1993), *Theatre and the World: Performance and the Politics of Culture*, London: Routledge.

The Bible. Authorized King James Version with Apocrypha (1997), Oxford: Oxford University Press.

Bigliazzi, Silvia, Peter Kofler and Paola Ambrosi (2013), 'Introduction', in Silvia Bigliazzi, Peter Kofler and Paola Ambrosi (eds), *Theatre Translation in Performance*, 1–26, New York: Routledge.

Bliss, Lee (1983), 'Defending Fletcher's Shepherds', *Studies in English Literature 1500–1900*, 23 (2): 295–310.

Bocchiola, Massimo (2015), *Mai più come ti ho visto: Gli occhi del traduttore e il tempo*, Torino: Einaudi.

Bogic, Anna (2010), 'Uncovering the Hidden Actors with the Help of Latour: The "Making" of *The Second Sex*', *MonTI*, 2: 173–92.

Bourdieu, Pierre (1984), *Distinction: A Social Critique of the Judgement of Taste*, trans. Richard Nice, New York: Routledge.

Boutwell, Brett (2012), 'Morton Feldman's Graphic Notation: *Projections* and Trajectories', *Journal of the Society for American Music*, 6 (4): 457–82.

Braden, Gordon (2010a), 'Tragedy', in Gordon Braden, Robert Cummings and Stuart Gillespie (eds), *The Oxford History of Literary Translation in English: Volume 2 1550–1660*, 262–79, Oxford: Oxford University Press.

Braden, Gordon (2010b), 'Comedy', in Gordon Braden, Robert Cummings and Stuart Gillespie (eds), *The Oxford History of Literary Translation in English: Volume 2 1550–1660*, 280–91, Oxford: Oxford University Press.

Braga Riera, Jorge (2009), *Classical Spanish Drama in Restoration English (1660–1700)*, Amsterdam: John Benjamins.

Brisset, Annie (1990), *Sociocritique de la traduction: Théâtre et altérité au Québec (1968–1988)*, Longueil: Les Éditions du Préambule.

Brockett, Oscar G., and Franklin J. Hildy (2003), *History of the Theatre*, 9th edn, Boston: Allyn and Bacon.

Brodie, Geraldine (2012), 'Theatre Translation for Performance: Conflict of Interests, Conflict of Cultures', in Rita Wilson and Brigid Maher (eds), *Words, Images and Performances in Translation*, 63–81, London: Continuum.

Brodie, Geraldine (2018a), *The Translator on Stage*, New York: Bloomsbury.

Brodie, Geraldine (2018b), 'Indirect Translation on the London Stage: Terminology and (In)visibility', *Translation Studies*, 11 (3): 333–48.

Brodie, Geraldine, and Emma Cole, eds (2017), *Adapting Translation for the Stage*, London: Routledge.

Brown, J. R., ed. (1995), *The Oxford Illustrated History of Theatre*, Oxford: Oxford University Press.

Bruni, Leonardo (1996), *Opere letterarie e politiche*, Torino: Utet.

Bulega, Franco (1984), 'La "fabula" tragicomica attraverso le polemiche sul Pastor Fido', *Comunicazioni Sociali*, 6: 47–68.

Butler, K. T. (1950), 'Giacomo Castelvetro 1546–1616', *Italian Studies*, 5 (1): 1–42.

Buzelin, Hélène (2006), 'Independent Publisher in the Networks of Translation', *TTR*, 19 (1): 135–73.

Caemmerer, Christiane (2013), 'Die Schäferliteratur und die Frauen', In John Pustejovsky and Jacqueline Vansant(eds), '*Wenn sie das Wort Ich gebraucht': Festschrift für Barbara Becker-Cantarino von FreundInnen, SchülerInnen und KollegInnen*, 221–47, Leiden: Brill.

Cameron, Derrick (2000), 'Tradaptation: Cultural Exchange and Black British Theatre', in Carole-Anne Upton (ed.) *Theatre Translation and Cultural Relocation*, 17–24, Manchester: St Jerome.

Canning, Charlotte (2013), 'Editorial: Looking Ahead', *Theatre Research International*, 38 (1): 1–4.

Carlson, Marvin (2001), *The Haunted Stage: The Theatre as Memory Machine*, Ann Arbor: University of Michigan Press.

Cary, Elizabeth (1994), *The Tragedy of Mariam the Fair, Queen of Jewry. With The Lady Falkland Her Life, by one of her daughters*, ed.Barry Weller and Margaret W. Ferguson, Berkeley: University of California Press.

Catford, John C. (1965), *A Linguistic Theory of Translation: An Essay in Applied Linguistics*, Oxford: Oxford University Press.

Cerratto-Pargman, Teresa, Chiara Rossitto and Louise Barkhuus (2014), 'Understanding Audience Participation in an Interactive Audience Performance', *NordiCHI '14: Proceedings of the 8th Nordic Conference on Human-Computer Interaction: Fun, Fast, Foundational*, 608–17, New York: ACM Digital Library.

Chaucer, Geoffrey (1988), *The Riverside Chaucer*, 3rd edn, Oxford: Oxford University Press.

Chesterman, Andrew (2009), 'The Name and Nature of Translator Studies', *Hermes*, 42 (13): 13–22.

Cicero, Marcus Tullius (1973), *Qual è il migliore oratore. Le suddivisioni dell'arte oratoria. I topici*, Milano: Mondadori.

Clubb, Louise George (1989), *Italian Drama in Shakespeare's Time*, New Haven: Yale University Press.

Connor, Rachel (2018), 'Retranslating Strindberg: Adaptation, (Re)location and Site-related performance', *Journal of Adaptation in Film & Performance*, 11 (1): 71–83.

Curran, Beverley (2007), 'Invisible Indigeneity: First Nations and Aboriginal Theatre in Japanese Translation and Performance', *Theatre Journal*, 59 (3): 449–65.

Cutchins, Dennis (2013), 'Bakhtin, Translation and Adaptation', in Katja Krebs (ed.), *Translation and Adaptation in Theatre and Film*, 36–62, New York: Routledge.

Daniel, Samuel (1606), *The Qveenes Arcadia. A Pastorall Trage-comedie* […] London: Simon Waterson.

Dávidházi, Péter (1993), 'Providing Texts for a Literary Cult: Early Translations of Shakespeare in Hungary', in Dirk Delabastita and Lieven D'Hulst (eds), *European Shakespeares: Translating Shakespeare in the Romantic Age*, 147–62, Amsterdam: John Benjamins.

De Marinis, Marco (1978), 'Lo spettacolo come testo (I)', *Versus*, 21: 66–100.

De Marinis, Marco (1979), 'Lo spettacolo come testo (II)', *Versus*, 22: 3–28.

Desmet, Christy, Sujata Iyengar and Miriam Jakobson (2019), *The Routledge Book of Shakespeare and Global Appropriation*, London: Routledge.

DeVito, Danny (1989), *The War of the Roses*, Gracie Films (U.S.).

Dobson, Michael (1992), *The Making of the National Poet: Shakespeare, Adaptation and Authorship, 1660–1769*, Oxford: Clarendon Press.

Donno, Elizabeth, ed. (1993), *Three Renaissance Pastorals: Tasso/Guarini/Daniel*, Binghamton, NY: Medieval & Renaissance Texts & Studies.

Douglas Home, William (1969), *The Secretary Bird – A Comedy*, London: Samuel French.

Douglas Home, William, and Marc-Gilbert Sauvajon (2019), *Le Canard à l'orange. Mise en scène de Nicolas Briançon. L'avant-scène théâtre*, 1456: 12–91.

Douglas Home, William, Marc-Gilbert Sauvajon and Nino Marino (1974), *L'anitra all'arancia: Due tempi di W. Douglas e M. Gilbert Sauvajon: Riduzione italiana di Nino Marino/Lo spettacolo è diretto da Oreste Lionello*, Rome: No publisher name.

Du Bellay, Joachim (1549), *La Deffence, et Illustration de la Langue Francoyse*, Paris: Arnoul L'Angelier.

Ducis, Jean-François (1827), *Oeuvres de J.F. Ducis. Tome Second*, Paris: Ladvocat.

Elam, Keir (1980), *The Semiotics of Theatre and Drama*, London: Methuen.

Even-Zohar, Itamar (2000), 'The Position of Translated Literature within the Literary Polysystem', 1st edn 1978, rev. edn 1990, in Lawrence Venuti (ed.), *The Translation Studies Reader*, 192–7, London: Routledge.

Farfan, Penny, and Ric Knowles (2011), 'Editorial Comment: Special Issue on Rethinking Intercultural Performance', *Theatre Journal*, 63 (4): no page numbers.

Fletcher, John (1609), *The Faithfull Shepheardesse*, London: R. Bonian and H. Walley.

Fois, Eleonora (2018), 'Theatrical Translation or Theatrical Adaptation? Staging *Noises Off* in Italy', *Journal of Adaptation in Film & Performance*, 11 (3): 241–57.

Frodella, Sheila (2012), 'La migrazione del *Pastor fido* in Inghilterra', in Fiorenzo Fantaccini and Ornella De Zordo (eds), *Studi di Anglistica e Americanistica. Percorsi di Ricerca*, Florence: Firenze University Press.

Ghini, Giuseppe (2017), '"L'eterna influenza francese": Classici russi per il tramite del francese all'alba del terzo millennio', *L'analisi linguistica e letteraria*, 25 (2): 159–74.

Gillespie, Stuart (2004), *Shakespeare's Books: A Dictionary of Shakespeare Sources*, London: Continuum.

Gilula, Dwora (1989), 'Greek Drama in Rome: Some Aspects of Cultural Transposition', in Hanna Scolnicov and Peter Holland (eds), *The Play out of Context: Transferring Plays from Culture to Culture*, 99–109, Cambridge: Cambridge University Press.

Gindt, Dirk (2013), 'Transatlantic Translations and Transactions: Lars Schmidt and the Implementation of Postwar American Theatre in Europe', *Theatre Journal*, 65 (1): 19–37.

Girshausen, Theo, ed. (1978), *Die Hamletmaschine: Heiner Müllers Endspiel*, Köln: Prometh Verlag.

Gostand, Reba (1980), 'Verbal and Non-Verbal Communication: Drama as Translation', in Ortrun Zuber (ed.), *The Languages of Theatre: Problems in the Translation and Transposition of Drama*, 1–9, Oxford: Pergamon Press.

Graham-Jones, Jean (2007), 'Editorial Comment: The Stakes of Theatrical Translation', *Theatre Journal*, 59 (3): no page numbers.

Graham-Jones, Jean (2017), 'The Critical and Cultural Fault Lines of Translation/ Adaptation in Contemporary Theatre', in Geraldine Brodie and Emma Cole (eds), *Adapting Translation for the Stage*, chapter 11, London: Routledge.

Grice, Paul (1991), *Studies in the Way of Words*, Cambridge, MA: Harvard University Press.

Guarini, Giovanni Battista (1590), *Il pastor fido* […] Venezia: G.B. Bonfadino.

Guarini, Giovanni Battista (1593), *Le Berger Fidelle, Pastorale. De l'Italien du Seigneur Baptiste Gvarini Chevalier*, Tours: Iamet Mettayer.

Guarini, Giovanni Battista (1602), *Il Pastor fido: or The faithfull Shepheard. Translated out of Italian into English*, London: Simon Waterson.

Guarini, Giovanni Battista (1623), *Le Pastevr Fidelle* […] *traduit d'Italien en vers François par Noble Antoine de Giravd* […], Paris: Claude Cramois.

Guarini, Giovanni Battista (1647), *Il pastor fido, The faithfull Shepherd. A Pastorall Written in Italian by Baptista Guarini* […] *And now Newly Translated out of the Originall*, London: R. Raworth.

Guarini, Giovanni Battista (1664), *Il pastor fido, The Faithful Shepheard. With an Addition of divers other Poems* […], London: A. Moseley.

Guarini, Giovanni (1666), *Il pastor fido. Le Berger fidelle* […] *En Vers François*, Paris: Gabriel Quinet.

Guarini, Giovanni Battista (1672), *Der Teutsch-Redende Treue Schaeffer des berühmten Welschen Guarini*, S.l.

Guarini, Giovanni Battista (1677), *Pastor Fido: Or, the Faithful Shepherd. A Pastoral. As it is Acted at the Duke's Theatre*, London: William Cademan.

Guarini, Giovanni Battista (2006–7), *El Pastor Fido de Battista Guarini. Ediciones de Nápoles 1602 y Valencia 1609*, trans. Cristóbal Suárez De Figueroa, ed. Enrique Suárez Figaredo, Madrid: Centro Virtual Cervantes.

Guarini, Giovanni Battista and Torquato Tasso (1591), *Il Pastor Fido* […]/*Aminta Favola Boschereccia*, London: John Wolfe.

Hale, Terry, and Carole-Anne Upton (2000), 'Introduction', in Carole-Anne Upton (ed.), *Theatre Translation and Cultural Relocation*, 1–13, Manchester: St Jerome.

Hand, Richard J. (2013), 'Half-Masks and Stage Blood: Translating, Adapting and Performing French Historical Theatre Forms', in Katja Krebs (ed.), *Translation and Adaptation in Theatre and Film*, 143–61, New York: Routledge.

Happé, Peter, and Wim Hüsken, eds (2016), *Staging Scripture: Biblical Drama, 1350–1600*, Leiden: Brill.

Hardwick, Lorna (2013), 'Translating Greek Plays for the Theatre Today: Transmission, Transgression, Transformation', *Target*, 25 (3): 321–42.

Hatim, Basil (1998), 'Text Politeness: A Semiotic Regime for a More Interactive Pragmatics', in Leo Hickey (ed.), *The Pragmatics of Translation*, 72–102, Clevedon: Multilingual Matters.

Hatim, Basil, and Ian Mason (1990), *Discourse and the Translator*, London: Longman.

Helou, Ariane Nada (2003), 'Translation and Performance of Greek Tragedy in the *Cinquecento*', MA thesis, University of California at Berkeley.

Hermans, Theo (1985), 'Images of Translation: Metaphor and Imagery in the Renaissance Discourse on Translation', in Theo Hermans (ed.), *The Manipulation of Literature: Studies in Literary Translation*, London: Croom Helm, 103–35.

Hermans, Theo (1999), *Translation in Systems: Descriptive and Systems-oriented Approaches Explained*, Manchester: St Jerome.

Heylen, Romy (1993), *Translation, Poetics & the Stage: Six French Hamlets*, London: Routledge.

Heywood, Jasper (1561), *The first Tragedie of Lucius Anneus Seneca* […] London: Henry Sutton.

Holland, Peter (1989), 'Space: The Final Frontier', in Hanna Scolnicov and Peter Holland (eds), *The Play Out of Context: Transferring Plays from Culture to Culture*, 45–62, Cambridge: Cambridge University Press.

Holmes, James S. (1988), *Translated! Papers on Literary Translation and Translation Studies*, Amsterdam: Rodopi.

Izzo, Carlo (1970), *Civiltà britannica*, Roma: Edizioni di storia e letteratura.

Jakobson, Roman (1959), 'On Linguistic Aspects of Translation', in R. A. Brower (ed.), *On Translation*, 232–9, Cambridge, MA: Harvard University Press.

Jeffs, Kathleen (2018), *Staging the Spanish Golden Age: Translation and Performance*, Oxford: Oxford University Press.

Jia, Hongwei (2017), 'Roman Jakobson's Triadic Division of Translation Revisited', *Chinese Semiotic Studies*, 13 (1): 31–46.

Johnston, David, ed. (1996a), *Stages of Translation: Essays and Interviews on Translating for the Stage*, Bath: Absolute Classics.

Johnston, David (1996b), 'Theatre Pragmatics', in David Johnston (ed.), *Stages of Translation: Essays and Interviews on Translating for the Stage*, 57–66, Bath: Absolute Classics.

Johnston, David (2000), 'Valle-Inclán: The Meaning of Form', in Carole-Anne Upton (ed.), *Theatre Translation and Cultural Relocation*, 85–99, Manchester: St Jerome.

Johnston, David (2011), 'Metaphor and Metonymy: The Translator-Practitioner's Visibility', in Roger Baines, Cristina Marinetti and Manuela Perteghella (eds), *Staging and Performing Translation: Text and Theatre Practice*, 11–30, Houndmills, Basingstoke: Palgrave Macmillan.

Johnston, David (2013), 'Professing Translation: The Acts-in-between', *Target*, 25 (3): 365–84.

Johnston, David (2015), *Translating the Theatre of the Spanish Golden Age: A Story of Chance and Transformation*, London: Oberon Books.

Karamitroglou, Fotios (2000), *Towards a Methodology for the Investigation of Norms in Audiovisual Translation: The Choice between Subtitling and Revoicing in Greece*, Amsterdam: Rodopi.

Keim, Katharina (1998), *Theatralität in den späten Dramen Heiner Müllers*, Tübingen: Max Niemeyer.

Kelly, L. G. (1979), *The True Interpreter: A History of Translation Theory and Practice in the West*, Oxford: Basil Blackwell.

Kennan, Patricia, and Mariangela Tempera, eds (1992), *Shakespeare from Text to Stage*, Bologna: CLUEB.

Kofler, Peter (2013), '"To Act, to Do, to Perform": Franz Heufeld's and Friedrich Ludwig Schröder's *Hamlet*-Adaptations for the German Stage', in Silvia Bigliazzi, Peter Kofler and Paola Ambrosi (eds), *Theatre Translation in Performance*, 180–96, New York: Routledge.

Kolpakova, Svetlana Georgievna, Veronika Lubimovna Gataullina and Ekaterina Vladimirovna Smyslova (2019), 'Historical and Political Allusions in the Drama "Hamletmachine" by Heiner Müller', *Journal of History Culture and Art Research*, 8 (4): 313–19.

Kowzan, Tadeusz (1970), *Littérature et spectacle dans leurs rapports esthtétiques, thématiques et sémiologiques*. Warsaw: Éditions scientifiques de Pologne.

Krebs, Katja (2007), *Cultural Dissemination and Translational Communities: German Drama in English Translation, 1900–1914*, Manchester: St Jerome.

Krebs, Katja (2013), 'Introduction: Collisions, Diversions and Meeting Points', in Katja Krebs (ed.), *Translation and Adaptation in Theatre and Film*, 1–10, New York: Routledge.

Kress, Gunther, and Theo van Leeuwen (2006), *Reading Images: The Grammar of Visual Design*, 2nd edn, London: Routledge.

Kyffin, Maurice (1588), *Andria: The first Comoedie of Terence, in English* [...], London: Thomas Woodcocke.

Ladouceur, Louise (2013), 'Surtitles Take the Stage in Franco-Canadian Theatre', *Target*, 25 (3): 343–64.

Laera, Margherita (2011), 'Theatre Translation as Collaboration: Aleks Sierz, Natalie Abrahami, Martin Crimp, Zoë Svendsen, Colin Teevan and J. Michael Walton discuss Translation for the Stage', *Contemporary Theatre Review*, 21 (2): 213–25.

Laera, Margherita (2019), *Theatre and Translation*, London: Red Globe Press.

Lambert, José (1993), 'Shakespeare en France au tournant du XVIIIe siècle. Un dossier européen', in Dirk Delabastita and Lieven D'Hulst (eds), *European Shakespeares: Translating Shakespeare in the Romantic Age*, 25–44, Amsterdam: John Benjamins.

Landers, Clifford E. (2001), *Literary Translation: A Practical Guide*, Clevedon: Multilingual Matters Ltd.

Lee, So-Rim (2018), 'Translation, Adaptation and Appropriation in Brook's *Mahabharata*', *Theatre Quarterly*, 34 (1): 74–90.

van Leeuwen, Theo (1999), *Speech, Music, Sound*, Houndmills, Basingstoke: Macmillan.

Lefevere, André (1977), *Translating Literature: The German Tradition from Luther to Rosenzweig*, Assen: Van Gorcum.

Lefevere, André (1980), 'Translating Literature/Translated Literature: The State of the Art', in Ortrun Zuber (ed.) *The Languages of Theatre: Problems in the Translation and Transposition of Drama*, 153–61, Oxford: Pergamon Press.

Lefevere, André (1992), *Translation, Rewriting, & the Manipulation of Literary Fame*, London: Routledge.

Lefevere, André (1998), 'Translation Practice(s) and the Circulation of Cultural Capital: Some *Aeneids* in English', in Susan Bassnett and André Lefevere (eds), *Constructing Cultures: Essays on Literary Translation*, 41–56, Clevedon: Multilingual Matters Ltd.

Lefevere, André (2000), 'Mother Courage's Cucumbers: Text, System and Refraction in a Theory of Literature', in Lawrence Venuti (ed.), *The Translation Studies Reader*, 233–49, London: Routledge.

Lei, Daphne P. (2011), 'Interruption, Intervention, Interculturalism: Robert Wilson's HIT Productions in Taiwan', *Theatre Journal*, 63 (4): 571–86.

Leppihalme, Ritva (2000), 'Foreignizing Strategies in Drama Translation: The Case of the Finnish *Oleanna*', in Andrew Chesterman, Natividad Gallardo San Salvador and Yves Gambier (eds), *Translation in Context: Selected Contributions from the EST Congress, Granada 1998*, 153–62, Amsterdam: John Benjamins.

Levin, Yuri D. (1993), 'Russian Shakespeare Translations in the Romantic Era', in Dirk Delabastita and Lieven D'Hulst (eds), *European Shakespeares: Translating Shakespeare in the Romantic Age*, 75–90, Amsterdam: John Benjamins.

Levý, Jiří (1969), *Die literarische Übersetzung: Theorie einer Kunstgattung*, Frankfurt am Main: Athenäum.

Levý, Jiří (2000), 'Translation as a Decision Process', in Lawrence Venuti (ed.), *The Translation Studies Reader*, 148–59, London: Routledge.

Levý, Jiří (2011), *The Art of Translation*, trans. Patrick Corness, Amsterdam: John Benjamins.

Link, Franz H. (1980), 'Translation, Adaptation and Interpretation of Dramatic Texts', in Ortrun Zuber (ed.), *The Languages of Theatre: Problems in the Translation and Transposition of Drama*, 24–50, Oxford: Pergamon Press.

Littau, Karin (2011), 'First Steps towards a Media History of Translation', *Translation Studies*, 4 (3): 261–81.

Liu, Siyuan (2007), 'Adaptation as Appropriation: Staging Western Drama in the First Western-Style Theatres in Japan and China', *Theatre Journal*, 59 (3): 411–29.

Lockwood, Dean P. (1918), 'Two Thousand Years of Latin Translation from the Greek', *Transactions and Proceedings of the American Philological Association*, 49: 115–29.

Machin, David (2009). 'Multimodality and Theories of the Visual', in Carey Jewitt (ed.), *The Routledge Handbook of Multimodal Analysis*, 181–90, London: Routledge.

Maitland, Sarah (2017), *What Is Cultural Translation?* London: Bloomsbury.

Manuwald, Gesine (2011), *Roman Republican Theatre*, Cambridge: Cambridge University Press.

Marinetti, Cristina (2013a), 'Translation and Theatre: From Performance to Performativity', *Target*, 25 (3): 307–20.

Marinetti, Cristina (2013b), 'Transnational, Multilingual and Post-dramatic: The Location of Translation in Contemporary Theatre', in Silvia Bigliazzi, Paola Ambrosi and Peter Kofler (eds), *Theatre Translation in Performance*, 27–38, London: Routledge.

Masson, Jean-Yves (2017), 'De la traduction comme acte créateur: raisons et déraisons d'un déni', *Meta*, 62 (3): 635–46.

Mateo, Marta Martinez-Bartolomé (1994), 'El nivel fonológico del lenguaje en el proceso de traducción', in A. Bueno García et al. (eds), *La traducción de lo inefable: Actas del Primer Congreso Internacional de Traducción e Interpretación de Soria*, 75–89, Soria: Colegio Universitario de Soria.

Mateo, Marta Martinez-Bartolomé (1997), 'Translation Strategies and the Reception of Drama Performances: A Mutual Influence', in Mary Snell-Hornby, Zuzana Jettmarová and Klaus Kaindl (eds), *Translation as Intercultural Communication: Selected Papers from the EST Congress – Prague 1995*, 99–110, Amsterdam: John Benjamins.

McCallum-Barry, Carmel (2004), 'Why Did Erasmus Translate Greek Tragedy?', *Erasmus Studies*, 24 (1): 52–70.

McElduff, Siobhán (2013), *Roman Theories of Translation: Surpassing the Source*, New York: Routledge.

Mee, Charles L. Jr (2007), 'I Like to Take a Greek Play', *Theatre Journal*, 59 (3): 361–3.

Meech, Anthony (2011), 'Brecht's *The Threepenny Opera* for the National Theatre: a 3p Opera?', in Roger Baines, Cristina Marinetti and Manuela Perteghella (eds), *Staging and Performing Translation: Text and Theatre Practice*, 126–38, Houndmills, Basingstoke: Palgrave Macmillan.

Meth, Jonathan, Katherine Mendelsohn and Zoë Svendsen (2011), 'Roundtable on Collaborative Theatre Translation Projects: Experiences and Perspectives', in Roger Baines, Cristina Marinetti and Manuela Perteghella (eds), *Staging and Performing Translation: Text and Theatre Practice*, 200–11, Houndmills, Basingstoke: Palgrave Macmillan.

Migne, J. P. (1859), *Patrologia Latina*, Vol. 22, Paris: J. P. Migne.

Minier, Márta (2013), 'Definitions, Dyads, Triads and Other Points of Connection in Translation and Adaptation Discourse', in Katja Krebs (ed.), *Translation and Adaptation in Theatre and Film*, 13–35, New York: Routledge.

Minutella, Vincenza (2013), *Reclaiming* Romeo and Juliet: *Italian Translations for Page, Stage and Screen*, Amsterdam: Rodopi.

Molinari, Cesare (1983), *Storia universale del teatro*, Milano: Mondadori.

Morini, Massimiliano (2006), *Tudor Translation in Theory and Practice*, Aldershot: Ashgate.

Morini, Massimiliano (2007), 'Shakespeare's Language and the Restoration', in Douglas A. Brooks (ed.), *The Shakespeare Apocrypha*, 339–88, Lewiston, NY: The Edwin Mellen Press.

Morini, Massimiliano (2013a), 'Virgil in Tudor Dress: In Search of a Noble Vernacular', *Neophilologus*, 97 (3): 591–610.

Morini, Massimiliano (2013b), *The Pragmatic Translator: An Integral Theory of Translation*, London: Bloomsbury.

Morini, Massimiliano (2013c), 'Towards a Musical Stylistics: Movement in Kate Bush's "Running Up That Hill"'. *Language and Literature*, 22 (4), 283–97.

Morini, Massimiliano (2020a), 'Luciano Bianciardi: Interventionist Translation in the Age of Mechanical Labour', *Target*, 32 (1): 123–43.

Morini, Massimiliano (2020b), 'Goths and Greeks: The Rise of Anglo-Saxon England and Germanic English in Early Modern Britain', *Filologia Germanica/Germanic Philology* 12: 171–90.

Morini, Massimiliano (2021), '"To reforme a frame": The 1602 Translation of Pastor fido and Elizabethan Theatrical Publishing', *Cahiers Élisabéthains*, 104 (1): 42–60.

Mounin, Georges (1965), *Teoria e storia della traduzione*, trans. Stefania Morganti, Torino: Einaudi.

Müller, Heiner (1995), *Theatremachine*, trans. Marc Von Henning, London: Faber and Faber.

Müller, Heiner (2003), *Manuscrits de* Hamlet-Machine, trans. Jean Jourdheuil and Heinz Schwarzinger, Paris: Les Éditions de Minuit.

Müller, Heiner (2012), *La macchina Amleto/Die Hamletmaschine*, trans. Karl Menschengen. No place of publication: Maldoror Press.

Müller, Heiner (2014), *Theater ist kontrollierter Wahnsinn: Ein Reader*, ed. Detlev Schneider, Berlin: Alexander.

Mullini, Roberta (2016), 'The Norwich Grocers' Play(s) (1533, 1565): Development and Changes in the Representation of Man's Fall', in Peter Happé and Wim Hüsken (eds), *Staging Scripture: Biblical Drama, 1350–1600*, 125–48, Leiden: Brill.

Mullini, Roberta and Romana Zacchi (2003), *Introduzione allo studio del teatro inglese*, 2nd edn, Napoli: Liguori.

Munday, Jeremy, ed. (2007), *Translation as Intervention*, London: Continuum.

Munday, Jeremy (2014), 'Using Primary Sources to Produce a Microhistory of Translation and Translators: Theoretical and Methodological Concerns', *The Translator*, 20 (1): 64–80.

Neri, Nicoletta (1963), *Il Pastor fido in Inghilterra, con il testo della traduzione secentesca di Sir Richard Fanshawe*, Torino: Giappichelli.

Newmark, Peter (1988), *A Textbook of Translation*, Hemel Hempstead: Prentice Hall.

Nolette, Nicole (2014), 'Le *Projet Rideau Project*: le théâtre "co-lingue", le bilinguisme officiel et le va-et-vient de la traduction', *Meta*, 59 (3): 654–72.

Nowra, Louis (1984), 'Translating for the Australian Stage (A Personal Viewpoint)', in O. Zuber-Skerritt (ed.), *Page to Stage: Theatre as Translation*, 13–21, Amsterdam: Rodopi.

O'Leary, Catherine (2018), 'Translating the Armed Struggle: Alfonso Sastre and Sean O'Casey in Spain', *Translation Studies*, 11 (1): 47–65.

O'Thomas, Mark (2013), 'Translation, Theatre Practice, and the Jazz Metaphor', *Journal of Adaptation in Film & Performance*, 6 (1): 55–64.

O'Toole, Emer (2013), 'Cultural Capital in Intercultural Theatre: A Study of Pan Pan Theatre Company's *The Playboy of the Western World*', *Target*, 25 (3): 407–26.

Oettinger, Anthony G. (1960), *Automatic Language Translation: Lexical and Technical Aspects, with Particular Reference to Russian*, Cambridge, MA: Harvard University Press.

Oittinen, Riitta (2000), *Translating for Children*, New York: Garland Publishing.

Olohan, Maeve (2017), 'Technology, Translation and Society: A Constructivist, Critical Theory Approach', *Target*, 29 (2): 264–83.

Parry, Graham (1990), 'A Troubled Arcadia', in Thomas Healy and Jonathan Sawday (eds), *Literature and the English Civil War*, 38–55, Cambridge: Cambridge University Press.

Pavis, Patrice (1992), *Theatre at the Crossroads of Culture*, London: Routledge.

Pavis, Patrice (2000), *Vers une théorie de la pratique théâtrale: Voix et images de la scène 3*, Villeneuve-d'Ascq (Nord): Presses universitaires du Septentrion.

Pavis, Patrice (2010), 'Intercultural Theatre Today', *Forum Modernes Theater*, 25 (1): 5–15.

Perron, Paul, and Patrick Debbèche (1999), 'Foreword', in Anne Ubersfeld, *Reading Theatre*, xiii–xx, Toronto: University of Toronto Press.

Pfeiffer, Kerstin, Michael Richardson and Svenja Wurm (2020), 'Translaboration in the Rehearsal Room: Translanguaging as Collaborative Responsibility in Bilingual Devised Theatre', *Target*, 32 (2): 358–79.

Pięta, Hanna (2019), 'Indirect Translation: Main Trends in Practice and Research', *Slovo.ru: baltijskij accent*, 10 (1): 21–31.

Pigman III, G. W. (2010), 'Pastoral Drama', in Gordon Braden, Robert Cummings, Stuart Gillespie (eds), *The Oxford History of Literary Translation in English: Volume 2 1550–1660*, 293–8, Oxford: Oxford University Press.

Plautus, Titus Maccius (1784), *Le commedie di M. Accio Plauto volgarizzate da Niccolò Eugenio Angelio col testo latino a dirimpetto*, Vol. X, Napoli: Vincenzio Mazzola-Vocola.

Polledri, Elena (2010), *Die Aufgabe des Übersetzers in der Goethezeit*, Tübingen: Narr.

Pozzi, Francesco (2006), 'La prima rappresentazione del Pastor Fido di Battista Guarini a Crema. Carnevale 1595 o 1596', *Insula Fulcheria*, 36: 265–82.

Prandoni, Marco (2019), 'Against Translation: The Struggle Over Translation for the Stage in the (Late) Dutch Golden Age', *InTRAlinea*, special issue on *Transit and Translation in Early Modern Europe*: 1–9.

Puttenham, George (1589), *The Arte of English Poesie* […], London: Richard Field.

Pym, Anthony (2009), 'Humanizing Translation History', *Hermes*, 42: 23–48.

Racz, Gregory J. (2019), 'Theatre', *Routledge Handbook of Literary Translation*, Chapter 19, London: Routledge.

Reiss, Katharina (1969), 'Textbestimmung und Übersetzungsmethode', in Wolfram Wilss (ed.) *Übersetzungswissenschaft*, 76–85, Tübingen: Max Niemeyer.

Reiss, Katharina and Hans J. Vermeer (1984), *Grundlegung einer allgemeinen Translationstheorie*, Tübingen: Max Niemeyer.

Reynolds, Bryan, ed. (2014), *Performance Studies: Key Words, Concepts and Theories*, London: Palgrave.

Robinson, Douglas (1991), *The Translator's Turn*, Baltimore: Johns Hopkins University Press.

Robinson, Douglas, ed. (1997), *Western Translation Theory from Herodotus to Nietzsche*, Manchester: St Jerome.

Robinson, Douglas (2017), 'What Kind of Literature is a Literary Translation?', *Target*, 29 (3): 440–63.

Rogoff, Gordon (1986), '*Hamletmachine* by Heiner Müller, Robert Wilson', *Performing Arts Journal*, 10 (1): 54–7.

Rose, Margaret, and Cristina Marinetti (2011), 'The Translator as Cultural Promoter: Or How Renato Gabrielli's *Qualcosa Trilla* went on the Road as *Mobile Thriller*', in Roger Baines, Cristina Marinetti and Manuela Perteghella (eds), *Staging and Performing Translation: Text and Theatre Practice*, 139–54, Houndmills, Basingstoke: Palgrave Macmillan.

Rousseau, Aloysia (2019a), 'William Douglas Home, le divertissement avant tout', *L'avant-scène théâtre*, 1456: 102–4.

Rousseau, Aloysia (2019b), '*Le Canard à l'orange* d'une rive à l'autre', *L'avant-scène théâtre*, 1456: 95–7.

Rozhin, Szczesna Klaudyna (2000), 'Translating the Untranslatable: Edward Redlinski's *Cud Na Greenponcie* [*Greenpoint Miracle*] in English', in Carole-Anne Upton (ed.), *Theatre Translation and Cultural Relocation*, 139–49, Manchester: St Jerome.

Salce, Luciano (1975), *L'anatra all'arancia*, Capital Films/Cinerix.

Sampson, Lisa (2003), 'The Mantuan Performance of Guarini's "Pastor Fido" and Representations of Courtly Identity', *The Modern Language Review*, 98 (1): 65–83.

Sánchez García, Encarnación (2019), '"Salientes acquae". Due edizioni poetiche napoletane in lingua spagnola: "El pastor fido" di Cristóbal Suárez (1604) e le "Obras" di Garcilaso de la Vega', in Andrea Baldissera (ed.), *Cancioneros del Siglo de Oro: Forma y formas/Canzionieri dei secoli d'oro: Forma e Forme*, 183–204, Como: Ibis.

Saudis, Elizabeth (2015), 'Palimpsestuous Phaedra: William Gager's Additions to Seneca's Tragedy for his 1592 Production at Christ Church, Oxford', in T. F. Earle and Catarina Fouto (eds), *The Reinvention of Theatre in Sixteenth-Century Europe: Traditions, Texts and Performance*, chapter 7, Abingdon: Legenda and Routledge.

Schechner, Richard (2013), *Performance Studies: An Introduction*, 3rd edn, London: Routledge.

Schlegel, August Wilhelm (1796), 'Etwas über William Shakespeare bey Gelegenheit Wilhelm Meisters', *Die Horen*, 6: 57–112.

Schleiermacher, Friedrich (1816): 'Über die verschiedenen Methoden des Übersetzens', *Abhandlungen der philosophischen Klasse der Königlich-Preussischen Akademie der Wissenschaften aus den Jahren 1812-1813*: 143–72.

Schlueter, Jane (2012), 'Samuel Daniel in Italy: New Documentary Evidence', *Huntington Library Quarterly*, 75 (2): 283–90.

Schott Syme, Holger (2012), 'Thomas Creede, William Barley, and the Venture of Printing Plays', in Martha Straznicky (ed.), *Shakespeare's Stationers: Studies in Cultural Bibliography*, 28–46, Philadelphia: Pennsylvania University Press.

Schultze, Brigitte (1987), 'Theorie der Dramenübersetzung – 1960 bis heute: ein Bericht zur Forschungslage', in Günter Ahrends (ed.), *Forum Modernes Theater*, Band 2, 5–17, Tübingen: Gunter Narr.

Schultze, Brigitte (1993), 'Shakespeare's Way into the West Slavic Literatures and Cultures', in Dirk Delabastita and Lieven D'Hulst (eds), *European Shakespeares: Translating Shakespeare in the Romantic Age*, 55–74, Amsterdam: John Benjamins.

Scolnicov, Hanna (1989), 'Introduction', in Hanna Scolnicov and Peter Holland (eds), *The Play out of Context: Transferring Plays from Culture to Culture*, 1–6, Cambridge: Cambridge University Press.

Senelick, Laurence (2007), 'Semper Fidelis', *Theatre Journal*, 59 (3): 369–72.

Serón-Ordóñez, Inmaculada (2013), 'Theatre Translation Studies: An Overview of a Burgeoning Field (Part I: Up to the Early 2000s)', *Status Quaestionis*, 5: 90–129.

Serón-Ordóñez, Inmaculada (2014), 'Theatre Translation Studies: An Overview of a Burgeoning Field (Part II: From the Early 2000s to 2014)', *Status Quaestionis*, 7: 28–73.

Serpieri, Alessandro et el. (1978), *Come comunica il teatro*, Milano: Rizzoli.

Serpieri, Alessandro (2002), 'Tradurre per il teatro', in Romana Zacchi and Massimiliano Morini (eds), *Manuale di traduzioni dall'inglese*, 64–75, Milano: Bruno Mondadori.

Serpieri, Alessandro (2013), 'Semantics and Syntax in Translating Shakespeare', in Silvia Bigliazzi, Peter Kofler and Paola Ambrosi (eds), *Theatre Translation in Performance*, 50–60, New York: Routledge.

Short, Mick (1996), *Exploring the Language of Poems, Plays and Prose*, Harlow: Longman.

Sidney, Philip (1966), *A Defence of Poetry*, ed. J. A. Van Dorsten, Oxford: Oxford University Press.

Simeoni, Daniel (1998), 'The Pivotal Status of the Translator's Habitus', *Target*, 10 (1): 1–39.

Snell-Hornby, Mary (1984), 'Sprechbare Sprache—Spielbarer Text. Zur Problematik der Bühnenübersetzung', in Richard J.Watts and Urs Weidmann (eds), *Modes of Interpretation*, 101–16, Tübingen: Narr.

Snell-Hornby, Mary (1988), *Translation Studies: An Integrated Approach*, Amsterdam: John Benjamins.

Snell-Hornby, Mary (1996), '"All the World's a Stage": Multimedial Translation – Constraint or Potential?', in Christine Heiss and Rosa Maria Bollettieri Bosinelli (eds), *Traduzione multimediale per il cinema, la televisione e la scena*, 29–45, Bologna: CLUEB.

Snell-Hornby, Mary (1997), '"Is This a Dagger Which I See Before Me?" The Non-verbal Language of Drama', in Fernando Poyatos (ed.), *Nonverbal Communication and Translation: New Perspectives and Challenges in Literature, Interpretation and the Media*, 187–201, Amsterdam: John Benjamins.

Spencer, Jenny (2007), 'Performing Translation in Contemporary Anglo-American Drama', *Theatre Journal*, 59 (3): 389–410.

Spregelburd, Rafael (2007), 'Life, of Course', *Theatre Journal*, 59 (3), 373–7.

Stevenson, Randall (2004), *The Oxford English Literary History. Volume 12/1960–2000. The Last of England?* Oxford: Oxford University Press.

Sticca, Sandro (1974), 'The "Christos Paschon" and The Byzantine Theater', *Comparative Drama*, 8 (1): 13–44.

Straznicky, Martha, ed. (2012), *Shakespeare's Stationers: Studies in Cultural Bibliography*, Philadelphia: Pennsylvania University Press.

Suárez de Figueroa, Cristóbal (2007), *El pastor fido*, ed. Enrique Suárez Figaredo, Fort Wayne, IN (Works of Miguel de Cervantes – https://users.pfw.edu/jehle/wcotexts.htm).

Suetonius, Gaius Tranquillus (1914), *Suetonius: with an English Translation*. London: Heinemann (The Loeb Classical Library).

Suvin, Darko (2001), 'On the Epistemology and Pragmatics of Intercultural Theatre Studies', in Günter Berghaus (ed.), *New Approaches to Theatre Studies and Performance Analysis*, 31–44, Tübingen: Max Niemeyer.

Terentius, Publius Afer (1989), *Le commedie*, Milano: Garzanti.

Totzeva, Sophia (1999), 'Realizing Theatrical Potential: The Dramatic Text in Performance and Translation', in Jean Boase-Beier and Michael Holman (eds), *The Practices of Literary Translation: Constraints and Creativity*, 81–90, Manchester: St Jerome.

Toury, Gideon (1995), *Descriptive Translation Studies – and Beyond*, Amsterdam: John Benjamins.

Tytler, Alexander Fraser (1907), *Essay on the Principles of Translation*, London: Dent.

Ubersfeld, Anne (1996a), *Lire le théâtre I*, 1st edn 1977, Paris: Belin.

Ubersfeld, Anne (1996b), *Lire le théâtre II. L'école du spectateur*, 1st edn 1981, Paris: Belin.

Ubersfeld, Anne (1999), *Reading Theatre*, trans. Frank Collins, Toronto: University of Toronto Press.

Upton, Carole-Anne, ed. (2000), *Theatre Translation and Cultural Relocation*, Manchester: St Jerome.

Upton, Carole-Anne (2011), 'The Translator as *metteur en scène*, with Reference to *Les aveugles* [*The Blind*] by Maurice Maeterlinck', in Roger Baines, Cristina Marinetti and Manuela Perteghella (eds), *Staging and Performing Translation: Text and Theatre Practice*, 31–48, Houndmills, Basingstoke: Palgrave Macmillan.

Venturi, Paola (2011), 'L'immobilità del traduttore: la traduzione dei classici moderni inglesi in Italia', PhD dissertation, University of Bologna.

Venuti, Lawrence (1995), *The Translator's Invisibility: A History of Translation*, London: Routledge.

Venuti, Lawrence (2013), *Translation Changes Everything: Theory and Practice*, Abingdon: Routledge.

Versényi, Adam (2007), 'Translation as an Epistemological Paradigm for Theatre in the Americas', *Theatre Journal*, 59 (3): 331–447.

Weaver, Warren (1955), 'Translation', in William N. Locke and A. Donald Booth (eds), *Machine Translation of Languages: Fourteen Essays*, 15–23, Cambridge, MA: Technology Press of the Massachusetts Institute of Technology.

Wiles, David (2007), 'Translating Greek Theatre', *Theatre Journal*, 59 (3): 363–6.

Wilson, N. G. (1973), 'Erasmus as a Translator of Euripides: Supplementary Notes', *Antike und Abendland*, 18: 87–8.

Winston, Jessica (2006), 'Early "English Seneca": From "Coterie" Translations to the Popular Stage', *Renaissance Quarterly*, 59 (1): 174–202.

Wolf, Alan J. (2011), 'Inferential Meaning in Drama Translation: The Role of Implicature in the Staging Process of Anouilh's *Antigone*', in Roger Baines, Cristina Marinetti and Manuela Perteghella (eds), *Staging and Performing Translation: Text and Theatre Practice*, 87–104, Houndmills, Basingstoke: Palgrave Macmillan.

Zatlin, Phyllis (2005), *Theatrical Translation and Film Adaptation: A Practitioner's View*, Clevedon: Multilingual Matters Ltd.

Ziosi, Antonio (2007), 'Seneca tragico nel Rinascimento europeo: tiranni, vendette, tombe e fantasmi tra novella e tragedia', in Delmo Maestri and Ludmilla Pradi (eds), *Matteo Bandello: Studi di letteratura rinascimentale*, 91–154, Alessandria: Edizioni dell'Orso.

Zuber, Ortrun, ed. (1980a), *The Languages of Theatre: Problems in the Translation and Transposition of Drama*, Oxford: Pergamon Press.

Zuber, Ortrun (1980b), 'Introduction', in Ortrun Zuber (ed.), *The Languages of Theatre: Problems in the Translation and Transposition of Drama*, xiii–xiv, Oxford: Pergamon Press.

Zuber-Skerritt, Ortrun, ed. (1984a), *Page to Stage: Theatre as Translation*, Amsterdam: Rodopi.

Zuber-Skerritt, Ortrun (1984b), 'Translation Science and Drama Translation', in Ortrun Zuber-Skerritt (ed.), *Page to Stage: Theatre as Translation*, 3–11, Amsterdam: Rodopi.

Zuber-Skerritt, Ortrun (1984c), 'Introduction', in Ortrun Zuber-Skerritt (ed.), *Page to Stage: Theatre as Translation*, 1–2, Amsterdam: Rodopi.

Zuber-Skerritt, Ortrun (1988), 'Towards a Typology of Literary Translation: Drama Translation Science', *Meta*, 33 (4): 485–90.

Zurbrugg, Nicholas (1988), 'Post-Modernism and the Multi-Media Sensibility: Heiner Müller's *Hamletmachine* and the Art of Robert Wilson', *Modern Drama*, 31 (3): 439–53.

Index

Lightning Source UK Ltd.
Milton Keynes UK
UKHW020209211022
410848UK00002B/66